Matthew Gage 1880s

PURSUING EDEN

Matthew Gage: His Challenges, Conquests and Calamities

By
Joan H. Hall

Coyote Hill Press
Camano Island, Washington

Reprint, 2023

Printed in the United States of America

ISBN #978-0-9912641-2-4

Published by
Coyote Hill Press
Camano Island, Washington

Edited by Richard A. Hanks, PhD
Cover, Layout & Design by Robin S. Hanks

CONTENTS

ILLUSTRATIONS - CREDITS

FOREWORD

Daughter of San Francisco; Chronicler of Riverside

An 1890 history of southern California wrote that those who built southern California were men who possessed "the genius to conceive and the courage to undertake and carry forward to completion gigantic schemes which advance the welfare of whole communities and are so far-reaching in their effects that their benefits cannot be computed." One of those men, they said, who was "first of this class," was Matthew Gage. The plains above Riverside, California were seemingly vast and arid; a prospective land in need of sustaining water. Gage judged it an obstacle but not a barrier to cross, after coming to Riverside in 1881. His vision and efforts would surpass his expectations and those of the pioneers who began to populate this crossover from desert land to one of plenty and a home to an inland empire.

Earlier works by Joan Hall chronicle the amazing and memorable architecture of the homes and impressive estates of these men and the area where she spent most of her life. Her later efforts came to focus on the people who gave Riverside the unique position it held in the history of Southern California. This effort may be her most significant contribution.

Efforts by Gage gave birth to the budding citrus industry of southern California by supplying the precious benefit of water. This book, by cherished local historian Joan Hall, can be seen as a sequel to her 1992 book, *A Citrus Legacy*, in which she examines the lives of her Great-grandfather Stephen Henderson Herrick and Grandfather Stephen Leonard Herrick. Pioneers of the area's citrus industry, they often partnered with Gage in the pursuit of an American Eden showcasing groves of tropical fruit overseen by a newly-created California aristocracy of wealthy investors and risk takers. In this work Joan has executed a deep dive into the herculean task Gage endured and how he overcame the obstacles to his goals and had the tenacity to persist in the face of such impediments. It is a story of a visionary, obsessed with his vision. Joan Hall's effort examines the detail of that vision which defined the future of Riverside.

"Mr. Gage has accomplished alone and unaided," wrote the 1890 history, "a work which for magnitude of achievement and beneficent results to society, is equaled by the life work of but few men…" Or few women, as well, including the remarkable contributions of Joan Herrick Hall.

Richard A. Hanks, PhD

PREFACE

This is an incredible story chronicling the triumphant accomplishments and frequent failures of a likeable, stubborn Irishman named Matthew Gage. It is a true story narrating his memorable decades living in Riverside, California and his quest to acquire 640 acres of useless desert land known as Section 30.

Matthew Gage's fame stemmed from building a unique irrigation canal that became the impetus to Riverside's title, "Home of the Navel Orange." Thousands of acres were planted in citrus trees and flourished because of the Gage Canal. Riverside was destined to be more of a paradise because of his canal system.

Matthew Gage was hailed an empire builder, a strong willed person who overcame difficulties and hardships that would have discouraged most men. There is little doubt as to Matthew Gage's fine qualities and his genuine love of family, his strong religious faith, and his zealous compelling ambitions. His riveting personality and jolly sense of humor generated sincere lasting friendships. Although he became a local hero, his ongoing lawsuits and legal battles evoked frequent criticism.

In Gage's search for justice and retaliation, many of his court cases were dependent upon pending adjudications that often involved years of litigation. Judicial proceedings were frequently postponed and, with the passage of time, details often were lost, forgotten, and forgiven. Ultimately, some longstanding legal suits were dismissed and Mr. Gage exonerated.

Basically, Matthew Gage's lack of funds was his misfortune and his downfall. He borrowed from various agencies and friends, anticipating significant returns would pay off and clear his debts. He failed, however, more than once, to recognize his obligations, neglecting repayment of principal and interest. Why he continued this humiliating and submissive practice, remains a mystery. Perhaps, he believed God would come to his rescue since he was a staunch Presbyterian and instrumental in founding Riverside's Calvary Presbyterian Church. Both friend and foe occasionally questioned his sense of jurisprudence and soundness of mind.

Historical events, both national and local, influenced the lives of Matthew Gage and his family as remote occurrences and unforeseen encounters altered their lives. Consequently, Riverside history is deep-rooted in this narrative and objectively reflects many inevitable joys and frustrations of the era. This is a true story of the auspicious life of Matthew Gage, of his devoted wife, Jane, and of their eight children, five of whom predeceased him.

History books and scholarly articles depict Matthew Gage as an ingenious developer, one of Riverside's most important pioneers. During the past few years, while researching this story, I formed a close, uncertain relationship with this charming, obstinate Irishman. There were times when I admired this visionary and other times when I wondered if he could not have been a mischievous, clever, charming rascal.

Joan Herrick Hall
2008

DESCENDANTS OF

James Gage = Margaret Jane Orr
1795-1852   1810-1892

Eliza Gage	Robert Gage	Matthew Gage	Sara Ann Gage	William John Gage
1839-1923	1841-1925	1844-1916	1848	1849-1917
m.	m.	m.	m.	m.
William Irving	Mary Irving	Jane Gibson	William Spooner	Mary Margaret Brough
1833-1904	1839-1932	1849-1929		1851-1913

Children of Matthew and Jane

i.   Margaret Jane Gage
      1870-1928

ii.   Edith Anna Gage
      1873-1881

                              (1) Henry Banks Henderson
iii. Maude Louise Gage m.   1874-
      1876-1956   (2) William Gage Irving
                                 1870-1941

iv.   Horace James Gage
      1880-1892

v.   Robert Condit Gage
      1883-1892

vi.   Anna Stewart Gage m. Henry Schuyler Montgomery
      1886-1955   1882-1963

vii. Frances Gibson Gage
      1887-1892

viii. Katherine MacKenzie Gage
      1889-1912

CHAPTER 1

Matthew Gage gained international fame for constructing a 20-mile-long irrigation system bearing his name. Many grew wealthy due to this enterprise although the ingenious developer himself lost several fortunes and struggled through years of litigation in an effort to remain solvent. During his lifetime, Gage and his wife lost five of their eight children, a colossal tragedy for devoted, loving parents. In 1881, he moved his family to southern California, hoping a milder climate would be beneficial for his frail seven-year-old daughter. As Matthew Gage gathered his brood for their departure, he had no realization that his ensuing years in Riverside, California, would give rise to celebrity notoriety for his exemplary achievements, however, at the same time, his integrity would be seriously questioned.

Eleven-year-old Margaret Jane Gage held Edith Anna's hand and helped her little sister climb up the steep step of the silent waiting train. She turned her face away as tears streamed down her cheek, not wanting school chums or her Irving cousins to see her cry. Family and friends wished the family God's speed and a safe journey. Her mother, Jane, held baby Horace and her father held five-year-old Maude's hand. The Gage family's great adventure was about to begin, moving thousands of miles from family and friends to a remote section in California. Departing proved to be a most difficult undertaking.

Matthew Gage said goodbye to his mother and to his brothers and sisters and their families, while Jane bid farewell to her parents and sisters. Leaving Kingston, Ontario, Canada, after so many years was an ordeal for the entire family.

With the future unknown, yet in high spirits, the family of six boarded a train for New York City where they transferred to the transcontinental *Union Pacific* that traveled cross-country to San Francisco. Six days on the noisy train proved tiresome, yet uneventful except for Edith's constant coughing. She coughed so hard one day, blood dribbled from her mouth, upsetting her sisters who cried at the scary sight. Matthew and Jane prayed that the warmer climate would help their daughter and relieve her frequent coughing spells.

Their destination was a new community in southern California named Riverside where several good friends had recently settled. Dr. Alfred Woodill, the kindly gentleman who had taken such good medical care of the expanding Gage and Irving families in Kingston, had enthusiastically recommended the milder winters in the new colony. Dr. Woodill, in poor health himself, had searched for a beneficial climate and settled in the inland town. People in Kingston commented that Matthew always followed his doctor's orders.

Other relocated Canadian friends in Riverside included the Jarvis brothers. Thirty-nine-year-old Joseph Jarvis, a medical doctor, arrived in Riverside in 1877 and, three years later, his younger brother, John, joined him. Together they invested in a citrus nursery business specializing in budding navel orange trees, a thriving and lucrative business in the new town.[1] Glowing letters to friends and relatives in Kingston conveyed their enthusiastic optimism and described their prosperous, healthy lives in "heaven on earth." Written communications between Kingston, Canada and Riverside, California took less than a week to reach their destinations.

Riverside, a planned colony, was established in 1870 by John Wesley North and associates, who had purchased several thousand acres of land south of San Bernardino. The founders organized the Southern California Colony Association and plotted a town, one mile square, near the Santa Ana River. An open ditch, nine miles long, supplied river water to the town. This water originated from annual rainfall and run-off from the snow in the surrounding mountains that covered hundreds of miles. Creeks and ditches flowed into the winding Santa Ana River, eventually emptying into the Pacific Ocean. This unfamiliar region was to be the Gage's new home where

Glenwood Cottage 1881

a milder, warmer climate would surely benefit little Edith Anna.

The Gage family arrived in Riverside on Saturday, March 26, 1881.[2] Will Hayt and his Concord coach transported the family and their meager belongings from the Colton train station ten miles northeast of town. When the coach came to a stop in front of the livery stable on Main Street, their good friends, Joseph Jarvis and Alfred Woodill, cheerfully greeted the tired, woebegone group. Each family member was welcomed by the congenial doctors as they stepped from the coach and set foot in the town of Riverside.

After glad tidings and friendly inquiries, the welcoming committee escorted the travelers across the dirt road to an unpretentious, two-story, frame building near the corner of Main and Seventh streets. The newcomers were informed that this was the Glenwood Cottage, home of the Miller family who welcomed guest boarders, especially families with young children. Matthew was assured that his family would be safe and comfortable staying in the Glenwood until he could locate suitable housing.

The raked dirt path leading to the entrance of the Glenwood Cottage was artistically edged in white rocks. Margaret and Maude stared at the strange looking greenery and cactus plants beyond the rocks, vegetation that they had never seen before. When the party entered the building, a hospitable young man immediately greeted them and Alfred Woodill quickly introduced Matthew to his Glenwood host, Frank Miller. The smiling 23-year-old Miller welcomed the Gages to Riverside and to his modest hotel where he lived with his family.

Dr. Woodill introduced other Miller family members including Frank's wife, Isabella, his sister, Miss Alice, and his mother, Mrs. Mary Miller. Fifteen-year-old Ed Miller, Frank's younger brother, was busy washing dishes and his father, Christopher Columbus Miller, was absent completing survey work for an out-of-town client. The Miller ladies invited Jane and the children to sit and visit in the dining room while the men conferred about accommodations. It was decided that the Gage family should occupy ground floor rooms for the convenience of the girls, who would share a room next to their parents. The rate for two rooms, including meals for the family, came to $7 a week.[3]

Joseph Jarvis invited the Gage family to Sunday supper the following day at the William Chaffey house on Adams Street. Other Canadians were invited, including former Kingston friends who had previously moved to Riverside. William Chaffey's brother, George Junior, and his father, George Senior, and their respective families lived together in the Adams Street house. William had married Hattie Jarvis, thus uniting two prominent Canadian families. Matthew was anxious to see the 20 acre orange grove that he and his brother, Robert, had purchased the year before, sight unseen. They had paid the Riverside Land & Irrigating Company $1,000 for the property located near California and Jackson streets. Their acreage contained 1,200 seedling orange trees, 700 apricot trees, 1,500 grapevines, and 200 cypress trees.[4] The

Chaffeys and Jarvises had recommended the investment and the Gage brothers trusted their friends advice and expertise.

Joseph Jarvis had first visited Riverside in 1877 when the new colony was seven years old. Born in Ontario, Canada, he and brother John attended school there and befriended fellow student, Matthew Gage. The three boys remained close friends. When Joseph returned to Canada, his enthusiastic reports of Riverside aroused the curiosity of both family and friends, including Matthew Gage who was eager to learn of its advantageous climate and promising investment opportunities.

Joseph Jarvis and Alfred Woodill spent the night at the Glenwood Cottage in lieu of traveling five miles, in the dark, to their homes in the Arlington area. Dr. Woodill owned a house and 20-acre orchard on Adams Street near the Jarvis home place. That evening the three men talked for hours, informing Matthew about local politics and recounting stories of successful people who had invested in real estate, especially grapevine and citrus tree property. Riverside's major crop was the cultivation of grapes, sun-dried for the raisin market, but citrus trees were gradually replacing poor producing vineyards.[5] He was delighted to know most citizens were God fearing, churchgoing folks who condemned the use of hard liquor and saloons. Matthew had many new concepts to consider, but remained confident of his future in Riverside, a new community that presented many opportunities.

Alice Miller and her mother, Mary, prepared a grand Sunday morning meal for their hotel guests. There were hungry mouths to feed with four of the six rooms occupied. Joseph hired a sizeable buggy for the Gage party. He and Alfred tied their horses to the rig and climbed aboard. The doctors were anxious to show-off their prosperous community and share innocent gossip with the new arrivals.

As they slowly trotted along Main Street, the first point of interest became a one-story structure identified as Roe's Drug Store. The doctor guides quickly announced it was more than a drug store due to its location in the center of town

5

Magnolia Avenue 1880s

and its congenial proprietor. Roe's store had become a general meeting place where people congregated and exchanged the latest news. The next point of interest was the one-story Blue Front Grocery Store, also on the west side of the street. The Gages were informed it was owned and operated by Frank Miller, who carried the best merchandise in town.

The congenial tour guides continued to point out landmarks as they slowly traveled along, turning onto dirt roads until they arrived at a broad boulevard the doctors called Magnolia Avenue. It was indeed wide, divided into two lanes separated by a strip of land in the middle. The girls in the back seats of the buggy pointed to strange looking trees with long necks, topped with fringe. Tall, skinny palm trees and weird shrubs with padded hands called cactus plants were strange sights to the Canadians. Dr. Woodill explained to Margaret and Maude that they must be very careful near cactus plants because the sharp spines were extremely painful.

As the buggy continued along the right side road, their attention was drawn to the opposite side where a citrus grove surrounded a new white clapboard building. The doctors informed the family it was the recently completed Magnolia

Avenue Presbyterian Church to be dedicated in two weeks. Matthew and his family had been active Presbyterians in Canada and he made a mental note of the upcoming date.

When they approached Jackson Street, the doctors pointed to Gage's property near the corner. Everyone, including little Horace, clapped their hands when they first viewed the well-maintained property. It was an exciting moment, an auspicious occasion for the Gage family to visit their own orchard covered with healthy fruit trees and vineyards. Even though the citrus trees were losing their blossoms, a sweet fragrance lingered in the air as they walked around inspecting the plantings.

The Chaffey family warmly greeted the Gages upon their arrival and made everyone feel welcome. The Gages were interested in the construction of the house, never having seen an adobe brick house. Built with thick walls, the three-year-old house contained six-rooms on the first floor and five small rooms upstairs.[6] Several generations occupied the place, including George Chaffey and wife Ann, their son William and his wife Hattie Jarvis, and their other son George, Junior, his wife Annette, and their sons, seven-year old Andrew and four-year old Ben.

Hattie was an excellent hostess, encouraging the Chaffey and Gage children to play outside in the huge front garden. While male guests gravitated to one another to share the latest business news, the ladies congregated around Jane, informing her where to shop for the best household items and latest fashions. The men discussed the many financial pitfalls of being a horticulturist but, at the same time, expressed hopes of increasing their citrus holdings. Matthew, with his witty Irish humor and a mischievous glint in his eye, was a most welcome addition to the Canadian alliance.

Matthew and Robert's Riverside property had been in the care of John Jarvis who managed other orchards for non-resident property owners. The Jarvis brothers operated a steam fruit dryer business in Arlington where they cured, packed, and annually shipped over four thousand pounds of fruit, primarily apricots. Matthew was anxious to learn more about his financial prospects for the upcoming orange and grape crops as he was committed to opening a business and getting his family settled in a comfortable home. He had aspirations of becoming prosperous and admired the achievements of his Canadian friends.

John Jarvis made some quick calculations and figured the Jackson Street property might realize approximately $2,500 from all crops if the unpredictable weather remained normal. Matthew calculated that half of this amount, after his brother's share, would be enough to establish his own business.

Several neighbors joined the Chaffey gathering, mostly Canadians who had settled near California and Adams streets.[7] This section of town was becoming known as the Canadian Tract, although it had been christened Arlington on December 18, 1880. Arlington, an English place name, originated from the Earl of Arlington, who had received a Virginia land grant in 1673. The name became increasingly popular after the Civil War with the establishment of the National Cemetery at Arlington, Virginia.[8] Land south of Riverside had previously been referred to as the Hartshorn Tract, the Sayward Tract, and the New England Colony. The city limits of Riverside encompassed the neighborhood community of Arlington.

After a full day of good fellowship and renewed friendships, Matthew drove his happy, tired family back to the Glenwood Cottage. He anticipated that the coming week would be filled with important decisions, foremost those involving a new business. He had faith in his ability and remained optimistic about his future in Riverside.

Early Monday morning, Matthew left his family at the Glenwood Cottage where he knew they would be safe and comfortable with the hospitable Miller family. His mission was to open a jewelry business as he was a qualified watchmaker and engraver with 18 years experience. He had successfully practiced his trade in Kingston and accumulated a small bank account, enough to open a small shop. Since his Canadian friends had mentioned Roe's Drug Store as a popular meeting place, he headed to the corner of Main and Eighth streets to make inquiries.

James Roe, with wavy hair and a shaggy, full beard, was rather an impressive man. Matthew found him well-educated and personable as they introduced themselves and became acquainted. They soon discovered they were the same age, both interested in good literature, and devoted members of their individual churches. Roe, a Baptist, was a deacon and sang in the choir. Due to his fondness for books, the friendly druggist provided space in his drug store where the public could rent or buy books from the library association.

Roe had been in Riverside since 1872, two years after the colony organized, and was recognized as an educated, influential citizen. He purchased 20 acres near the corner of Riverside and Central avenues where he planted a grove of seedling orange trees. As a knowledgeable and controversial figure, he became seriously concerned with the community's water issues and, consequently, established a local newspaper, *The Riverside Press*, in order to voice his protesting opinions.[9]

Matthew realized Roe's Drug Store was the most desirable location in town and the ideal place to begin his new venture. After a lengthy conversation, Matthew agreed to rent space in a small corner where he could open his jewelry business repairing clocks and watches. Part of his limited baggage, when he left Kingston, included a fine set of small tools, expressly for working with quality jewelry. James Roe was a likeable character and people gathered in his store to pass the time of day and hear the latest news and gossip. No newspaper, however, could match the ongoing news that circulated within Roe's Drug Store.

Two days before Matthew opened his jewelry business, customers at Roe's were discussing the latest rumors of a large land sale. The Riverside Land & Irrigating Company sold 12,000 acres in and around the Arlington area for $100 an acre to Samuel C. Evans and other investors. Evans, a retired banker from Indiana, had settled in Riverside where he paid

$120,000 for the land plus 1200 shares of water stock in the Riverside Canal. The water stock was appurtenant to the acreage and the noteworthy transaction was legally recorded in the San Bernardino County Recorder's office. Townspeople were elated with the news. With prospects for future growth in the area, everyone anticipated development would surely increase the value of their own property.

On April 9, 1881, less than two weeks after his arrival in Riverside, Matthew Gage opened his new business in the south corner of Roe's Drug Store. He was grateful for the space because the great demand for commercial rentals commanded high rates. He sent to San Francisco for new merchandise in anticipation of future expansion. With his family comfortably residing at the Glenwood Cottage, he conscientiously directed his time and energy to his profession. With his well trimmed goatee, full head of red, curly hair, pleasing personality, and a superior business location, he soon became well-known, well-liked, and successful.

On Sunday, April 25, 1881, the Magnolia Avenue Presbyterian Church was dedicated to serve all Riverside Presbyterians. The impressive, wooden building faced Magnolia Avenue and cost $3,500. Church pews were originally rented to defray additional expenses. Ten charter members, who lived near-by and represented pioneer families, were instrumental in founding the church.[10] The Gage family attended the ceremonial service and afterwards returned to the Glenwood Cottage, exhausted from the long, bumpy drive. Regardless of their discomfort from the dusty, uncomfortable road, Matthew and Jane agreed that the children would certainly benefit

Magnolia Ave. Presbyterian 1881

from the teachings of the Bible and consequently planned for the family to attend church whenever possible.

Working at Roe's Drug Store proved an interesting experience for Matthew. News of illnesses, accidental mishaps, visiting relatives, and changes of weather were pleasantly exchanged. This idle talk managed to filter and scatter around the valley and Matthew became privy to firsthand news, some bizarre and some ordinary. Due to his friendly personality, the 37-year-old became well acquainted with drug store customers. His relationship with Frank Miller, who worked next door in his Blue Front Grocery Store, evolved into a lasting friendship. Both young men were religious, assertive, and ambitious, destined to become distinguished Riverside citizens.

The warm hospitality bestowed upon the Gage family by Frank Miller and his wife and mother, made the worrisome move from Canada an easier transition. Isabella, Frank's wife, had been a school teacher before her marriage and she took a special interest in Margaret and Maude. She offered the girls easy lessons in arithmetic and encouraged them to read books from her small library. While the girls appeared happy in their new surroundings, Edith Anna continued to be sickly and listless. Nevertheless, Matthew and Jane were encouraged when Frank Miller and Isabella concurred that Riverside's climate would surely benefit seven-year-old Edith Anna.

During the Gage family's residence in the Glenwood Cottage, Frank Miller's father, Christopher Columbus Miller, was working out-of-town on an immense surveying project for Thomas Blythe, a San Francisco land developer. Blythe was constructing an irrigating system for a vast land development west of the Colorado River.[11] C. C. Miller had successfully surveyed the route of Riverside's lower water canal in 1871 and was highly regarded for his precise engineering skills. Like Blythe, Matthew soon became aware of the vital importance in acquiring water for improving dry, useless land.

While working at the store one day, Matthew met a young man named Frank Green who was seeking a buyer for his house. His new house on Fifth Street was nearly completed and he was anxious to move closer into town. Mr. Green wished to dispose of his house and grove located on Fourteenth Street and Roe's Drug Store seemed the logical place to seek a buyer. Matthew asked many questions relating to its size and condition and was motivated to inspect the house the same day. That afternoon he rode his horse to Frank Green's place near the southeast corner of Fourteenth and Mulberry streets and discovered a handsome two-story, clapboard house with a wide side porch and tall brick chimney. A long driveway edged in stout eucalyptus trees stretched beyond the gabled house ending at a large barn located near the back of the property. A dormant vegetable garden and empty chicken coops stood nearby. The property had no need of a windmill as it was located below the original Riverside Water Canal.

Matthew decided it would be an ideal place for his family home and conferred with Frank and Hattie Green about renting the property until he established his jewelry

Matthew Gage House near Mulberry and 14th Street

business. They reached an agreement whereby Matthew could rent the house with the option to purchase when he became financially able. Ten acres of producing citrus trees, and a variety of fruit trees were included in the agreed asking price of $5,400. The Greens were moving in two weeks and the Gage family could move into the Fourteenth Street house the first of May.

That evening Matthew surprised his family with the announcement that they would soon be moving. He described the house, with its citrus grove and barn, and said he would send for their furniture and trunks in Kingston the next day. Maude asked question after question including whether she could have a dog. Margaret asked if she could have her own room and timid Edith Anna questioned where she would sleep. Little Horace just clapped his hands since everyone seemed so happy.

Jane became emotional, tears rolling down her face, at the thought of living in her own house surrounded in orange trees. The prospect of becoming a citrus grower gave Matthew added satisfaction because the family could supplement their income from the sale of the fruit crop. When news of the Gage family's move to Fourteenth Street reached their Riverside Canadian friends in Arlington, they were disappointed not to have the family as neighbors.

On the first day of May, the family moved into their new home. Frank Miller and family were sad to see them leave the Glenwood Cottage but promised to visit one another often. Margaret, Maude, Edith, and little Horace raced through the rooms of their new home, cheering and laughing as they inspected each and every room. Margaret and Maude shared a large upstairs bedroom and Edith had her own small room due to her disturbing cough. Baby Horace slept on a child's cot in a large closet near his parent's room.

When Matthew's fine leather books arrived, they were carefully placed in the family's glass-front bookcases. Jane's treasured spinet was proudly positioned in the front parlor.

Good literature and melodious music would fill the Gage household for more than four decades.

The adjacent citrus grove appeared to have been irrigated and maintained by Frank Green. It was determined that the vegetable garden and the chicken coops could be revitalized with a little work. With no piped water south of the original mile square of town, the family relied on canal water channeled into their small reservoir. Neighbors across the street received piped water, but the Gage house was located just out of the mile square.[12] Everyone in the family settled into their new surroundings with little difficulty and, in no time, the Gages became prominent citizens.

While the family was still getting settled, Riverside's Canadian and British subjects celebrated Queen Victoria's 63rd birthday on May 24th. As Queen of Great Britain and Ireland, she was honored in Riverside every year on her birthday. English flags hung from windows and were draped over porches as her loyal subjects gathered for picnics and celebrations. The Gages were still getting settled and didn't participate in celebrating the Queen's birthday that year. Nevertheless, they draped a Union Jack flag from a second story window to honor the Queen.

Matthew's jewelry store was 10 blocks from home, an easy walk or bicycle ride. Margaret and Maude occasionally rode their bicycles to deliver warm mid-day meals to their father. The girls were thrilled to enter the store where so many strangers seemed to know one another and everyone appeared friendly to their father. From time to time, Jane, asked the girls to bring some item home from the Blue Front Grocery where Frank Miller recorded the purchase, placed it on a tab, and allowed Matthew to settle the account at the end of the month.

Three times a week, Chinese vendors stopped at the Gage house with their wagons filled with fresh vegetables and unfamiliar Chinese items. After asking her Canadian friends about some of the strange appearing produce, she introduced Chinese cabbage and squash to her family meals.

Lychie nuts became a special treat for auspicious occasions. During summer months, wagons were covered with tent-like overhangs to protect the produce and, on really hot days, moist gunny-sacks covered the freshly picked vegetables. In winter, when vegetables were difficult to grow, the Chinese wagons were filled with bags of coal and bundles of firewood for sale.[13]

Jane was proud of her renewed vegetable garden, where she grew potatoes, beets, and turnips for her family. Diversified planting between rows of orange trees was a common practice, but she refrained from planting watermelons or pumpkins for she had read that their roots would draw moisture from the trees. Chickens were allowed to roam freely through the grove where they consumed troublesome grasshoppers. The cow needed milking, the garden needed weeding, and there were enough daily chores for everyone.

Matthew was a welcome addition to Riverside, a churchgoing man who stood against strong drink and belonged to Good Templars. Lodge members met at the public hall at Ninth and Main streets where, on June 11, 1881, Matthew presented a short temperance address on "The evil demons of drink." The fund-raising event raised $36, a lodge donation for the organ fund of the Magnolia Avenue Presbyterian Church.

As business continued to grow, Matthew purchased a safe to store his valuable merchandise. Summer in Riverside was a new experience for the Canadian family when temperatures reached 90 degrees or more. Many townspeople escaped to cooler mountain climates or beach areas where they camped among the trees or sandy shorelines. Edith Anna's health had not improved with the dry, hot weather or from the variety of medicines that Doctor Alfred Woodill had prescribed. Doctor Joseph Jarvis, who specialized in women's and childhood diseases, was spending more time developing property than practicing medicine, but he regularly sent Matthew the latest reports concerning consumption.[14]

Nationally-known doctors were prescribing a change of climate for patients wasting away from consumption. They recommended that the best places for invalids were Florida, Italy, and southern California. The San Bernardino Valley, with nearby deserts, was considered a health resort with beneficial sanitariums. Physicians believed that the most healthful conditions for patients predisposed to consumption were dryness, warmth, sunshine, and equality of temperature. On August 29, 1881, just months after moving to Riverside, Edith Anna Gage died, age seven years, nine months, and fourteen days. The cause of her death was later recorded at Olivewood Cemetery as tuberculosis meningitis, not consumption.

The entire community sympathized with the grief-stricken family. A simple funeral took place at the Gage residence with Reverend Robert Condit presiding. Condit was a guest preacher at Magnolia Avenue Presbyterian Church. Matthew and Jane decided not to bury their beloved Edith in Riverside's only cemetery. Evergreen Cemetery was in a deplorable state, occupied by legions of ground squirrels and gophers. Little Edith Anna Gage was laid to rest in the orange grove adjacent to the Gage house. The family had sentimentally named their property, My Sweet Anna, in memory of Edith Anna.

CHAPTER 2

As the young community prospered, so did Matthew Gage. In October 1881, he paid N. H. Kingsley $800 for a deep lot on Main Street next to Roe's Drug Store. He then sent measurements of the lot to his older brother Robert, a talented architect living in Kingston. Robert Gage designed Matthew's one story, brick building containing two individual stores. Before the end of the year, contractors Sheldon & Munsell were busy building the $2,000 structure.[1] Matthew Gage and other merchants were anticipating a lucrative winter tourist season.

Matthew expanded his line of merchandise and began advertising in both local newspapers, the *Riverside Press* and the *Press & Horticulturist*. His newspaper notices featured "a fine assortment of gold, steel, and rubber spectacles, eyeglasses, and shades. Powerful lenses for miners and fruit growers are available along with fine gold watches and charms." He was busy early in December selling Christmas gifts in need of engraving. That season, a fashionable trend for fancy ladies' pocket and pin-on watches, was even more fashionable because of Matthew's ability to add personalized, engraved initials. His business had flourished beyond his expectations and the limited space in Roe's store soon became inadequate. Much of his success was due to his pleasing personality and cheerful outlook on life. He always found time to visit with friendly customers and appeared interested in their activities.

Noteworthy news that December had to do with his friends, George and William Chaffey. They had purchased a thousand acres of barren land, with water rights, near the foothills of the Sierra Madre Range, west of San Bernardino. Captain J. S. Garcia, a retired Portuguese seaman, sold them the property for $1,500. Subsequently, the Chaffeys purchased additional acreage and subdivided it into ten-acre blocks,

Chaffey Family Home

with water delivered to the highest corner of each plot. In this venture the brothers followed the advice of Luther C. Holt, a scholarly authority on water disputes, who had been involved in Riverside's earlier water controversies. Chaffey's system eliminated land owner disputes over water rights. They strongly advocated "water and land should never be separated" and supported the 1876 Satterwaite Act providing, "once water was furnished to land, it became appurtenant to that land, a perpetual easement."

The innovative Chaffeys had also developed a process to seal the canals by cementing the V-shaped wooden flumes with a mixture of concrete, systematically tamped into the form, and onto the slopping sides. While the mixture remained soft, four holes were poked through making small openings for metal gates that could adjust the flow into furrows. Cementing canals, although expensive, reduced water seepage and became economically effective.

To attract Canadian and eastern investors, the brothers named their new settlement the Etiwanda Colony. Etiwanda had been the name of an Indian chief who once roamed the shores of Lake Michigan. Etiwanda acreage was priced at $200 to $300 an acre and sold within eight months. The Chaffey brothers realized huge profits, high acclaim and good publicity.[2]

Matthew followed each stage of the Chaffey's Etiwanda project, amazed at their stalwart work and long term vision. The brothers assumed significant financial risks, tackled unfamiliar problems, and reaped good benefits for their efforts.³ Matthew deliberated over his capability to attempt such a complicated enterprise.

In December, Frank Miller remodeled and enlarged his Blue Front Grocery Store. The 25-foot wide building of brick and adobe, was extended to a depth of 125-feet and the interior was enhanced with additional shelves, enclosed by sliding glass windows and a new coat of paint. After the remodeling was completed, the enlarged front window displayed several sets of fine china and popular glassware.⁴

Frank A. Miller

Matthew Gage and Frank Miller, owners of adjoining buildings under construction, joined forces and installed a stone sidewalk in front of their stores. They received many compliments for their undertaking, especially from dignified ladies forced to shop in the rain. Riverside's rainy season extended from October to April, with an annual rainfall averaging about ten-and-a-half inches.

The Gage family's first winter in southern California proved to be cold, windy, and rainy. On January 11, 1882, Riverside experienced a perfect day with clear skies and sunshine. During the night, the mercury dropped to 26 degrees and snow began to fall. The unexpected snowstorm continued for 24 hours, with eight inches of snow covering the ground.⁵ Citrus growers used long sticks to shake heavy snow accumulated on tree branches that would otherwise split and break under the increased weight. In spite of the unconventional snowstorm, the yearly rainfall that year was a mere three inches, far below average. Matthew Gage and his family realized it was not a typical winter and they were content, and dedicated, to remain in Riverside where they had many good friends and enjoyed a respectable Christian life.

Gage's Grand Opening took place on February 4, 1882, when citizens throughout the area were invited to visit and inspect his new building and jewelry store. It was divided into two separate stores, the largest occupied by Kelsy Brothers, dealing in gentlemen's clothing, with one corner devoted to Miss Johnson's Millinery. Gage's Jewelry Store occupied the smaller front store with J. M. Drake's News Depot located in the back room where he carried a full line of music, periodicals, and magazines. For his grand opening, Matthew purchased a variety of gold and silver watches and an assortment of fine jewelry. In his front window stood a decorative, ebony cabinet filled with traditional silverware and tasteful stationary.[6] The Gage children, Margaret, Maude, and Horace, were dressed in their finest Sunday clothes and politely greeted visitors to their father's new building. It was a proud day for the entire family.

On March 4, 1882, one month after opening his new jewelry store, Matthew launched an ambitious enterprise drastically changing his life. The Desert Land Act of 1877 provided that a person could acquire a section of land, 640 acres, for 25 cents an acre if reclaimed by irrigation within a three-year period.[7] He filed a claim to Section 30, in Township 2, South of Range 4, West of San Bernardino Meridian, in the United States Land Office in San Bernardino, the county seat. Section 30 located two miles east of downtown Riverside, near Box Springs Mountain, encompassed the area between Eighth Street, (University Avenue) Chicago Avenue, Canyon Crest Drive, and Le Conte. Under the Desert Land Act, Section 30 was designated as desert land because crops of no value had ever grown there.

Matthew first heard about Section 30 from James Roe whose former minister, Reverend C. F. Forbes of Riverside's Baptist Church, resigned his pastoral duties in June 1879. He had moved from Riverside and abandoned his claim to Section 30. Matthew became interested in acquiring such a large tract, especially after witnessing the successful developments of the Chaffey brothers. Barren land was considered worthless without water but Matthew believed he could obtain water from flowing springs and wells located in the nearby Box Spring Mountains. Jane and the children were overjoyed with the prospects of Matthew's challenging project and the bright future it offered.

Their congenial family physician, Alfred Woodill and his family, moved from Arlington to a convenient downtown location closer to his many patients. He named his two-story cottage near Twelfth and Lemon streets Scotia Place, in honor of his native Nova Scotia. Its roomy dining room, with a separate side-porch entrance, was converted into an examining room with an adjoining office. This likable, popular doctor, with a multitude of patients and friends, maintained a lifetime friendship with Matthew Gage.

The two visited often with their homes, My Sweet Anna and Scotia Place, just blocks apart. When Matthew mentioned filing a claim to Section 30, Alfred Woodill enthusiastically encouraged him and contributed funds for a preliminary survey. Matthew respected his friend's constructive suggestions and sound advice. Alfred Woodill's scholarly knowledge and keen insight into reclaiming Section 30 strengthened Matthew's motivation to build an irrigation canal. With the application of water, the 640 fertile acres in Section 30 would sell for high prices.

Reports had circulated for years about the existence of natural flowing springs in the Box Spring Mountains where early stagecoaches stopped to water their animals. Therefore, Matthew Gage obtained an option to purchase a portion of Section 32, on condition that an ample water supply could be procured. After lengthy investigations, and hundreds of borrowed dollars, he found the existing springs inadequate to reclaim Section 30.

Matthew concluded that the most reliable information pertaining to water involved the 1880 survey conducted by William Hamilton Hall, a state water engineer. He had supervised a crew that surveyed potential water supplies east of Riverside for future reservoirs. Headwaters from Warm Creek and the Santa Ana River were reported as good sources, capable of irrigating the plains east and south of town. Hall concluded that a reasonably sized reservoir, supplied by a number of water ditches and the Santa Ana River, would produce a sufficient amount of water to irrigate hundreds of acres. Qualified engineers, and the general public, believed the idea impossible and little attention was originally given to Hall's survey.[8]

Nevertheless, Matthew studied the survey in detail. He estimated that such an irrigation system would cost between $375,000 and $450,000, or about $30 an acre, and could service 15,000 acres. Matthew analyzed and scrutinized the Hall report, attempting to apply its conclusions to his Section 30. While continuing to search for an adequate water supply, the actions of his friends captivated his attention. To Matthew's surprise, 34-year-old George and 26-year-old William Chaffey began developing another community west of their Etiwanda Colony.

In 1882, they established the new town of Ontario, located along the base of the Sierra Madre Mountain Range with a water supply from nearby streams and a generous subterranean flow. Ontario became a celebrated model colony featuring a wide, divided boulevard, Euclid Avenue, resembling Riverside's Magnolia Avenue. Land sold quickly due to an efficient distribution of water, provisions for an agricultural college, and deed restrictions forbidding the sale of intoxicating liquor. Inspired by the Chaffey's success, Matthew continued his search for available water.

Jane Gage had lived in Riverside for nearly a year when she expressed a desire to own their Fourteenth Street home. Consequently, on March 20, 1883, Matthew paid Frank and Hattie Green $5,400 for Lot One of the Southern California Colony Association, consisting of ten acres with improvements.[9]

Due to Matthew's successful jewelry business, the family was able to hire a Chinese houseboy named John, the standard name for most Chinese men. He wore a skinny pigtail down his back, shirttails outside his trousers, and a smile on his face. Matthew provided John living quarters in the barn, one large room with an outside door. Jane was finding the upkeep of the two-story house more difficult, even though she occasionally hired house servants. The petite, energetic lady was pregnant for the fifth time. Margaret, age 12, Maude, age 6, and Horace, age 2, had daily chores. Although the girls helped around the house, they most often spent time playing with Queenie, their big, shaggy dog.

Several months after buying the Fourteenth Street house, Matthew sold his jewelry business to John Law of Puget Sound. Law's move to Riverside, and the milder climate, was prompted by his wife's poor health.[10] The Puget Sound Newspaper highly recommended Law as "a thoroughly reliable businessman and a desirable citizen." Although Matthew sold his business, he remained owner of the building and collected rent. With only two years remaining to reclaim Section 30, the 39-year-old former jeweler seriously pursued his options.

For more than a year Matthew had followed the work of J. Alphonso Carit, owner of some 2,800 acres of land situated on the Santa Ana River near the old town of San Bernardino. Known as the San Bernardino Artesian Basin, part of the property consisted of an alluvial bench south of the river, with a large portion situated in the river bottom. This outlying property was considered good artesian land with healthy cottonwoods, willows and grasses, positive evidence of underground water. This potential water supply was located 12 miles from Section 30.

Drying Grapes for Raisins in Riverside

Carit had purchased most of the acreage in 1871 from Mr. Conn and the following year he acquired the Welles family ditch for $4,500. The conveyance stated: "the real property and all water, water right, and water privileges to said lands is conveyed to J. A. Carit, his heirs, and assigns forever."[11] The Santa Ana River ran through Carit's land for three miles with access to available water from both banks.

As an absentee owner, he had leased portions of the dry plains to tenant farmers who grew alfalfa and raised sheep. In 1881, he moved from San Francisco to San Bernardino hoping that the drier climate might improve his wife's failing health. At about the same time that the Gages had moved to Riverside, Alphonso Carit began taking a greater interest in his vast holdings. He acquired major water interests in the Carlton Ditch, Warm Springs, and the Hunt and Cooley ditch, consisting of important water rights near the Santa Ana River. Matthew recalled William H. Hall's 1880 survey outlining various junctions and his reference of Warm Springs as a prime water source. By June, Carit conveyed artesian water to portions of his dry mesa land by use of trenches and furrows, a process most encouraging to Matthew.

In the summer of 1883, he befriended Alphonso Carit, an interesting character born in France who had lived in Central America before moving to San Francisco and then to San Bernardino. He informed Gage that the vineyards near Bordeaux, France were selling for as much as $16,000 an acre. French vineyards annually produced much smaller crops than California. Consequently Carit discussed the possibility of setting out his own vineyards for wine or raisins. He envisioned converting his useless land into productive agricultural use with water from the Santa Ana River and his artesian wells. Matthew was intrigued with J. Alfonso Carit and his visionary theories and the two congenial gentlemen forged an unexpected friendship.

The Gage family experienced their first earthquake on a Saturday evening about 8:30 that September. The first jolt extended across Los Angeles and San Bernardino counties and was relatively light. The second shock quickly followed and was much heavier. About three minutes later, a third jolt hit. At this point everyone ran outside into the street, silently frightened. For a few minutes no one said a word and when the earth settled down, they laughed and loudly applauded. There would be other earthquakes during their lifetime in California but the family would always remember their first big shake.

A hotly contested issue surfaced in the fall of 1883 when a group of local men voted to incorporate the City of Riverside. Numerous land owners opposed this movement, however, fearing higher taxes and continuing poor management of the Riverside Canal Company. Nevertheless, a united campaign in favor of incorporation stressed the need for licensing saloons and controlling the marketing of liquor. With a population of 3,000, many citizens believed that the time had come to establish a municipal government.

Matthew Gage, in favor of incorporation, delivered a lengthy address at a grand rally in the recently completed

Pavilion. The box-shaped structure stood on the northwest corner of Seventh and Main streets, opposite the Glenwood Cottage Hotel, and was first known as the Citrus Fair Pavilion. Built by public subscriptions, it housed religious gatherings, public entertainments, and civic meetings. In March 1882, Riverside's fourth Citrus Fair was held there and Helen Hunt Jackson, a correspondent for Scribner *Century Magazine*, visited the fair and inspected varieties of locally grown citrus fruit.[12]

Citrus Fairs had started in 1878 as neighborhood gatherings for farmers to exhibit varieties of their homegrown fruit. They first met in their homes where they displayed their finest citrus fruits to be judged as to good appearance and flavor. In 1881, after the Gage family moved to Riverside, local citizens acquired property for a larger meeting place and exhibition hall. The Pavilion, constructed two feet off the ground, included an elevated stage for lectures and a variety of programs.

Before the grand rally for incorporation began, a company of uniformed men paraded through the streets of downtown carrying torches to announce the free rally at the Pavilion. The building filled with interested spectators who attentively listened to Matthew Gage's comments about the City of Riverside.

> Frequently it becomes necessary for individuals to sacrifice personal feelings and sentiments for the public good. If the settlement is to be benefited in the main by incorporation, the people should favor such a move, even though they might see objections, real or fancied. The temperance idea is one that should interest us all. The right to control the liquor business is recognized all over the country. If government could control the manufacture and sale of the toy pistol, could it not control the whiskey business that is something more than toy pistols? Another purpose of incorporation is the water question. We hail the water right as sound as

anything can be but its control should be in a different shape. The Riverside Canal Company has outlived its usefulness.[13]

On this momentous day, September 15, 1883, Matthew Gage and John Greenleaf North, future adversaries, favored incorporation. It was the first and last time they would ever agree on any issue.

In September 1883, citizens of Riverside voted to incorporate with 228 votes cast in favor and 147 against. Matthew Gage was ineligible to vote, however, for only American citizens had that right. His son, Robert Condit Gage, born that year, automatically became a citizen of the United States. Robert was named for his uncle, Robert Gage, and his middle name may have been derived from the surname of the minister, Reverend F.M. Condit, serving Magnolia Presbyterian Church.

For a short period Margaret and Maude attended the Sixth Street School, at Lime Street, that had been enlarged from its original four rooms to six rooms in order to accommodate grades up to eight. On election day the girls came home early quite frustrated about incidents at their school. Someone had broken into classrooms, defaced the walls and destroyed their desks. There seemed to be no correlation between the senseless ransacking and the incorporation vote, bewildering students and teachers as to the motives behind such purposeless destruction.

Beautiful California was being advertised in the east as never before. *The Central and Southern Pacific Railroad's* organized low-priced excursions for groups or individuals including luxury sleeping cars, comfortable tourist cars and men's smoking cars. In the fall a large California excursion, filling five Palace cars, arrived in Los Angeles with former governor of Iowa, Samuel Merrill, his wife, son and maid on board. Later, Mr. Merrill visited Riverside and was pleased with the community and its prospects.

In January 1884, 66-year-old George Chaffey, Sr., died and was buried in the new cemetery in Ontario, California. His sons, William and George Jr., were living in the Garcia ranch house in Etiwanda, where they had successfully sold most of their property. Chaffey siblings, Dr. Elwood, Charles, and Emma continued to live in the Riverside homestead on Adams Street until the end of the year when George Chaffey Jr. sold it and 20 acres for $16,000. Even though Matthew and Jane missed the proximity of the lively Chaffey families, they remained close friends for many years

On January 15, 1884, Matthew signed a $4,000 promissory note, mortgaging his ten-acre homeplace to George Crawford, a fellow Canadian living in Arlington. It was a five-year note with 12 percent interest due semi-annually. This may have been the beginning of his deleterious routine of borrowing money even though similar transactions were common practice among businessmen during the 1880s. The following year George Crawford assigned the same promissory note to Matthew's neighbor, A. J. Twogood. Several months later Twogood assigned the same note to Cornelius Jensen, who died later that year. Then, the executrix of Jensen's estate sued Matthew Gage for the whole sum. Five years later the demand was finally satisfied and paid in full, including an additional $400 attorney fees.[14] Matthew continued borrowing money from various sources apparently convinced that water on Section 30 would make him a rich man and thereby settle all debts.

From July 1882 through June 1883, less than three inches of rain was recorded in Riverside. There had been little rainfall for the past three years. Matthew noted that the Santa Ana River remained a peaceful brook during the summer months but could run high and become destructive in the winter. In the winter of 1883-1884, Riverside and all of southern California experienced periods of record-breaking rainfall.

During December and January a few inches of rain were accompanied by heavy winds. Early settlers often said that the wind was caused by "leaving open the gate in the Cajon Pass." When it started raining in early February, everyone welcomed the "golden drops." The following week snow began to fall, covering lofty peaks of surrounding mountains. Then heavy rains began and continued hard and steady. Between a Thursday night and a Sunday night, it rained four inches bringing the season total to 14 inches.

Due to the force of the intensive downpour, mud and boulders rolled off saturated hillsides and mountains, falling into the Santa Ana River. The river filled rapidly, overflowed its banks, and carved out new embankments. Residents living along the entire length of the Santa Ana River reported the crashing sounds of heavy boulders tumbling end over end down the river towards the ocean. Heavy rains destroyed railroad bridges, cut off communications, and left Riverside isolated from the outside world.

Canals overflowed and streets became rivers of mud. Rushing water, six feet high, roared down the Tequesquite Arroyo as it flowed westward towards the Santa Ana River. Melting snow added to the volume of the river and uprooted trees were carried downstream. Surging water removed large sections of land along both sides of the river. Citrus crops and vineyards were badly damaged or completely destroyed. Riverside's rainfall in February measured nearly eight inches, in March six-and-a-half inches, and the season total reached a record 23 inches.

It was during this extraordinary rainy winter that Samuel Merrill, former governor of Iowa, visited Riverside due to comments from his good friend Stephen H. Herrick who had stopped there the previous year seeking museum artifacts to replace collections destroyed by a cyclone at Grinnell College. When Herrick reported to Grinnell trustees about his acquisitions, he also praised the town of Riverside as attractive and progressive. Furthermore, he claimed the residents to be good Christian people opposed to liquor and saloons. Consequently, when Mr. Merrill visited southern California, Riverside topped his itinerary.[15]

After returning to Grinnell, Iowa, Samuel Merrill encouraged business associates and friends to organize a syndicate to invest in inexpensive railroad land near the town of Riverside. They intended to develop an adequate water supply for dry lands and to sell the property for sizable profits. The businessmen incorporated the Iowa Land and Improvement Corporation and obtained a one-year option to portions of Sections 5, 7, 17 and 19, located northeast of Section 30. *The Southern Pacific Railroad* agreed to sell the Syndicate 2,183 acres for $20,200.[16]

Samuel Merrill made inquiries to determine if adjacent property owners would be interested in obtaining water to irrigate their dry land for one-half of their acreage. This offer, a common agreement among water providers, was considered to be a fair proposition as water increased the value of land ten fold or more. The majority of property owners, however, were not interested in the proposition, especially coming from out-of-state promoters, thus the Iowa people temporarily abandoned their project. Unexpected inquiries by Iowa investors concerning water delivery put extra pressure on Matthew Gage to accelerate his search for water. The Iowans had far greater resources than Gage and with their combined corporate capital, he believed that they would easily acquire rights-of way.

Real estate continued to change hands as tourists and settlers purchased producing orchards and vineyards, capitalizing on Riverside's fertile soil and ideal growing conditions. Franciscan and Jesuit Missionaries had introduced the grape, apricot, plum, and peach to California and shown native converts how to dry fruit in the sun. Sun dried fruit required little labor as warm, sunny days did most of the work. Riverside farmers cultivated a plump Muscat grape imported from France and, in time, the town became known as the center of California's raisin industry. The raisin grape was the only one raised in the community, a temperance town opposed to the manufacture or consumption of wine.

During spring and summer months, growers tended their vines as clusters of grapes grew larger and matured. In September Indian families arrived from the desert areas, on foot and horseback, looking for work picking grapes. Clusters, carefully cut from the vine, were placed on wooden pallets raised an inch off the ground between rows of vines. These trays held 20 to 25 pounds of grapes that were dried into raisins. After several weeks they were dried, cleaned and placed in storage to be packed. Fancy packed raisins sold for $2.50 a box. With normal weather conditions, one acre of grapes could return $100 to $200 annually. Weather governed the success of a crop, especially grapes.[17]

In the afternoon of August 23, 1884, black clouds began to gather over the southeastern horizon of town. Pattering drops of rain soon began falling and increased quickly in volume. The intensity of the storm swelled as white balls of hail bounced off the ground. Heavy rain flooded streets turning them into rivers of mud; irrigation canals overflowed, pouring additional water across the landscape. The Santa Ana River rose three feet, windmills collapsed in the wind, basements flooded and roofs leaked. The three-mile wide storm swept through town creating a path of destruction. Rain turned into large hailstones that plunged into the ripening grapes, bursting them open, rendering them useless. The once-a-year grape crop was ruined and many vineyards were subsequently replaced with citrus trees, primarily with the popular navel orange variety. The demand for Riverside's navel orange, a seedless, firm textured winter fruit, was on the rise and an acre of oranges returned three times as much as an acre of grapes. An exhibit of Riverside navel oranges won first prize at the New Orleans 1884 Exposition and marked the beginning of California's great industry.

Matthew accelerated his efforts to locate water. He spent more time around Carit's tract, southeast of the county seat of San Bernardino. The Santa Ana River ran through Carit's undeveloped mesa containing numerous springs, ditches and artesian wells. Matthew continued to trudge over the property with a small leveling instrument to determine if a gravity flow canal was indeed practical.

Not trusting his nonprofessional calculations, he hired Christopher Columbus Miller, an experienced engineer, to survey the terrain to determine the feasibility of building such a canal. Carit's tract to his Section 30 involved 12 miles of uneven terrain and the grade of gravity flow had to be exact. After several weeks of substantial examinations, and many calculations, Mr. Miller implied a canal could be accomplished and reasoned that the numerous artesian wells on the Carit property could provide additional sources of water. With artesian wells, proper water rights, and strategically placed reservoirs, C. C. Miller concluded that an intricate canal system could be devised to irrigate Section 30.

This was the best possible news for Matthew. He enthusiastically shared Miller's surveying outline with Alfred Woodill as the two men seriously studied the report and made plans to proceed. The most important issue depended on purchasing Carit's tract, including all his water rights, and secondly, to obtain rights-of-way through private lands for the construction and maintenance of an irrigation canal. However, little business was conducted during the usually hot month of August when many families left town seeking cooler climates in the mountains or beach communities.

During the month churches closed and most ministers left town. However, one minister told his congregation, "The devil remained as busy as ever, because he was accustomed to hot weather and hence needed no vacation." On a mild August Sunday, Matthew took his family to the Carit Tract near San Bernardino for a picnic. When Margaret, Maude, and Horace jumped from the buggy, they were amazed to see magic fountains spouting water high into the air. Jane explained the artesian wells were pressured underground and forced the water to the surface, but the children were not convinced. They happily jumped through the waterspouts most of the day. Matthew told his children that a giant underground tub or basin held an ocean of water from decades of rain and

Artesian Wells of Gage Canal

melted snow. He further explained that he hoped to use some of the "liquid gold" to irrigate Section 30.

Later that month, after weeks of planning and legal maneuvering, J. Alfonso Carit agreed to sell his land to Matthew Gage. He had decided to return to San Francisco where a number of excellent clinics had previously helped his ailing wife. Her health had not improved in the southern California climate. The two men signed an option agreement whereby Matthew Gage agreed to purchase 2,800 acres of land and all associated water rights and privileges belonging to J. Alfonso Carit within a year. Part of the deed read:

> Twenty-acre surveys, 640 acres, 900 acres, 560 acres and 700 acres, including all water rights and appurtenances and incidental privileges. Also fence on south side of railroad and all growing crops and wood chopped on premises.[18]

Matthew paid an option fee of $5,000, took possession of the property, and Carit kept title to the land until the entire $175,000 price was paid. Matthew, elated with prospects of a good water supply, had one year remaining to claim Section 30 and one year to buy the Carit tract.

CHAPTER 3

During the summer of 1884, Europe was experiencing a severe cholera epidemic and foreign tourists gravitated to the United States. Riverside's Glenwood Cottage received a modest share of European vacationers all year. One day Frank Miller invited Matthew Gage to meet an English guest and introduced him to Wilson Crewdson, a London financier who was on his honeymoon. Crewdson informed them of his fascination and pursuit of Oriental art and recounted his travels and acquisitions for British museums.

During a prior conversation with the distinguished Englishman, Frank Miller shared the story of Matthew Gage's endeavor to obtain water to reclaim Section 30. The English gentleman had little knowledge of agriculture or the importance of water. Nevertheless, he and Matthew ultimately spent hours evaluating methods of water distribution and the logic of gravity flow. During their time together, Matthew did not mention specific possible sources of water.

Wilson Crewdson had influential banking connections with Price, Waterhouse & Company, the prestigious international accounting firm. Although he offered to invest in Gage's canal, Matthew respectively declined, preferring not to involve outside parties in his proposed canal.[1]

Matthew's engulfing enthusiasm, embracing Section 30, spread throughout the family as they looked forward to financial security and a lifestyle enjoyed by the Chaffey families. He informed his children of his busy schedule in the coming months but assured them that when the canal was completed the family would have enough money to do as they pleased.

On October 6, 1884, Christopher Columbus Miller began surveying potential routes from water sources to various points along the mesa. Miller hired his son-in-law, G. O. (Olivo) Newman, a Swedish civil engineer and his brother,

(Hjalmer) Otto Newman, to assist in the survey work. Otto Newman worked as a chainman for 16 days during which time dozens of survey spikes were visible a mile above the Riverside Water Company canal.

Ideal October weather greeted the survey party as they hiked along the uneven terrain and foothills east of town. C. C. Miller concluded a variety of tunnels would be necessary in order for water to pass through certain precipitous bluffs. After several weeks of work, his preliminary report indicated that a functional irrigation ditch was indeed feasible. Furthermore, a canal could begin near Warm Springs and extend to Section 30, a distance of some 12 miles.[2]

When Matthew had confirmation that a canal could be built to Section 30, he quietly began to secure rights-of-way from property owners along the proposed route. He contacted each owner, offering to provide an inch of water to every five acres in return for $100 per acre or a deed conveying one half of their acreage. Payment to obtain water was to be secured by a mortgage on the land, with payments extending over a five-year period at eight percent interest. His offer was essentially the same as that offered previously by Samuel Merrill. The option read:

> To Matthew Gage, I quitclaim right-of-way and right-to-entry to 100-foot strip of land for construction and maintenance of a canal for irrigating purposes primarily, also all right-of-way for lateral ditches from said canal through land.

Clauses in various contracts stated that he reserved the right to develop additional water resources and "to sell such water." When necessary, a sentence was added including "right-to-bridge over canal."[3]

Matthew had little trouble securing mortgage contracts from property owners and his acquisitions kept the San Bernardino County Recorder's office busy recording deeds, agreements and rights-of-ways contracts.

Gage Brothers
left to right - William John, Robert and Matthew

A shortage of funds continued to be a problem for Matthew and he subsequently traveled to Kingston, Canada, to interest family and friends to invest in his venture. At the time, economic conditions in Canada and around the world were unfavorable due to the decline in commodity prices. Accordingly, banks became unstable and investment money scarce. Matthew assured his brothers that the land in Section 30 would be worth $500 an acre when water was applied, enabling him to repay all loans with interest. William John and Robert Gage could only offer their brother token loans. Matthew desperately needed $175,000 to close the deal with J. Alfonso Carit.

On his return to Riverside he made a spur-of-the-moment decision and traveled to Des Moines, Iowa to confer with Samuel Merrill. He was a desperate man who needed to strike a deal with the Iowa Syndicate, owners of land northeast of his Section 30. He was eager to convince them that he could also provide the water to their property. His proposal to supply water in return for an advance cash payment was a common contract. After meeting with board members of the Iowa Syndicate, Chairman Merrill expressed disinterest in his proposition and Matthew returned to Riverside empty handed.[4]

The Riverside Banking Company, headed by O. T. Dyer, advanced a modest loan to Matthew, primarily due to the mortgages he held on lands yet to receive his canal water. He continued with preliminary work, sinking and capping artesian wells for future use. At the time few appeared interested in his undertaking, except for his family and his good friend, Dr. Woodill.

Heavy rainfalls during the winter of 1884-1885 enhanced fresh, new growth to magnolia and pepper trees lining Magnolia Avenue. Impressive homes and mansions built along the Avenue for well-to-do newcomers were surrounded by colorful flower gardens and citrus groves. Handsome and personable Henry Lockwood, and his wealthy mother, Mrs. LeGrande Lockwood, built a two-story mansion on the corner of Madison and Magnolia avenues and named it, Casa Blanca, "white house" in Spanish. Young Lockwood organized the Casa Blanca Tennis Club and built two dirt tennis courts next to his house.[5] This recreational organization evolved into an elite social club where Riverside's finest ladies and gentlemen enjoyed afternoon tea.

Rains also benefited numerous cypress hedges encompassing new mansions and orange groves along Magnolia Avenue. Whenever Matthew Gage drove the family to Sunday services at the Magnolia Avenue Presbyterian Church, they commented on the healthy, maturing trees bordering the impressive boulevard. When Matthew was out-of-town, Jane seldom attended church because of the long, dusty drive and difficulties in handling their buggy. In its place, Jane read the Bible to her children and played their favorite hymns on her spinet.

The winter rains were helpful to the navel orange crop, producing good sized fruit and outstanding flavor. Most new groves were planted to navel orange nursery stock, often referred to as the Washington Navel Orange or Riverside Navel Orange. Growers began receiving good crop returns from their maturing trees and demand for oranges increased as winter visitors publicized Riverside's prime fruit. Matthew, ever alert and energetic, envisioned his Section 30 covered in navel orange trees, a virtual oasis and the pride of Riverside.

Canadian and British subjects celebrated Queen Victoria's 66th birthday in May. The Gage family joined their Canadian friends in Arlington for a festive picnic and a day of celebration. The happy occasion concluded with everyone singing "Happy Birthday To You" and "Hail to the Queen."

A few months later, Riverside paid tribute to the 18th President of the United States, Ulyssess Simpson Grant, who had died near Saratoga, New York on July 23, 1885. People throughout the nation held memorial services in his honor. Riverside businesses closed so that citizens could attend an afternoon memorial program held in the Pavilion. The Gages joined the Woodill and Jarvis families. After the ceremony, the men discussed the subject of becoming United States citizens and agreed that citizenship offered certain advantages.

During the spring, rolling hillsides of the Santa Ana Canyon blossomed with bright multi-colored wildflowers. The dirt road through the canyon was edged in eucalyptus trees imported from Australia and planted as windbreaks to protect citrus trees from damaging wind. Wood from the imported trees supplied both firewood and building material. During the hot summer months, many Riverside families used this canyon road to reach beach cities.

In August, Matthew loaded a Concord wagon with tents and camping equipment and drove the family through the Santa Ana Canyon, headed for Laguna Beach.[6] Margaret was 15 years old, Maude, nine, Horace, five, and Robert, two. They traveled over the winding canyon road, camping the first night in Tustin, near the Santa Ana River. The following day, they arrived at Laguna Beach Canyon and joined 50 other campers. Matthew pitched their two tents near 85 other tents scattered among the shade trees. After getting his family settled, Matthew returned to Riverside where important business awaited him. He was pleased his family could enjoy the cooler coastal climate while camping among good Riverside friends.

During the summer of 1885, Matthew signed an agreement with six owners of the Camp Carlton ditch, an essential right to Santa Ana River water. Under terms of the agreement, ditch owners allowed Matthew to move diversion water upstream where the flow could enter his proposed canal. In return, he offered to provide a continuous flow of 130 miner's inches for six days of every month from May through November.[7] Camp Carlton had been named for a Civil War Union Army Troop that once camped on the site. Matthew would be entitled to all the flow in the river in excess of that delivered to the Camp Carlton ditch.

Matthew also purchased a six-sevenths interest in the Hunt-Cooley Ditch in San Bernardino, a long established water right to all surface flow of the Santa Ana River at a certain location. J. Alfonso Carit owned the other one-seventh interest in the ditch. Heavy rains in 1884 had cut a deep channel near the Hunt-Cooley Ditch allowing water to flow through the Carit land, thus creating 500 inches of water where no water had flowed before. Matthew had deeper trenches installed to increase the volume of water. While he spent most of his time working at the Carit Tract, he depended on John, his Chinese laborer, to care for his home place and adjacent citrus grove.

John, a reliable worker, efficiently maintained the Fourteenth Street property, irrigating the grove and tending the grounds. He was a typical member of Riverside's Chinese population, consisting of single men who worked in vineyards, groves, or as house servants. Chinese men also operated wash-houses in makeshift shacks on rented land downtown near Ninth and Orange streets. Here, they washed clothes in nearby open ditches making the water dirtier for

Riverside's Chinatown Near Tequesquite Arroyo

users down the line. In June 1885, a local newspaper took up the hot campaign to remove all Chinese from downtown, stating that "Chinatown wash houses breed disease right in the middle of town and are keeping and selling whiskey in violation of city ordinances."[8]

Subsequently, the Board of Trustees passed an ordinance to prevent the further erection of wooden buildings in downtown Riverside, a move to eliminate any building in the Chinese quarters. The owner of the Chinatown property notified his tenants to vacate within 30 days after October 1, or rent would increase to $500 a month. After many meetings, the Chinese residents agreed to move from downtown to a remote location in the Tequesquite Arroyo, near the Santa Ana River, where they would not be disturbed. Even though John was not a regular visitor to the new Chinatown, he always joined his countrymen there to celebrate Chinese New Year.

Matthew continued to improve his water supply, adding numerous springs and artesian wells, attaining

Adoniran Judson Twogood

338-inches from springs and 189 inches from the Hunt and Cooley Ditch. He hired C. C. Miller again, this time to make precise measurements concerning the amount of available water derived from the Hunt and Cooley Ditch. Ambrose Hunt and George Cooley accompanied Mr. Miller, serving as witnesses to his work and independently recorded his measurements and findings. Miller's documentation may have been Gage's means to obtain additional loans to finance his work, but in future years it became important evidence in a powerful lawsuit.

Matthew Gage had failed to raise enough money from his Canadian friends and relatives in order to pay Carit in September 1885. The need to close the deal was paramount and his only hope of obtaining Section 30 was to convince the Iowa Syndicate that he could deliver a substantial supply of water to their land in return for cash.

Near the end of August, Matthew invited A. J. Twogood to accompany him to Iowa. This time he arrived with legal contracts, drawn by several Riverside attorneys and reviewed by William and George Chaffey. Matthew hoped Mr. Twogood, on friendly terms with the Iowa men, could convince them of his good intentions.

Finally on August 27, 1885, legal, binding contracts, approved by both of their attorneys, were signed by Matthew Gage and Samuel Merrill. In addition, Gage furnished a certificate of water measurements, compiled by surveyor C. C. Miller and witnessed by Hunt and Cooley, to the Iowa Syndicate.

Matthew agreed to build a canal, for irrigation purposes, starting near San Bernardino, with a permanent and sufficient water supply to be delivered to portions of Sections 5, 7 and 17 by August 1, 1886. Within five years after August 1, 1886, he also agreed that the canal would be cemented, on the bottom and sides, to the south boundary of the Syndicate's property. The contract further stated:

> To deliver a permanent and sufficient supply of water, 335 inches, with a good water title, free from all encumbrances. Water would be delivered on a basis of one inch of water to five acres, measured under a four-inch pressure. Said canal would be supplied with waters from the Santa Ana River, springs, and water rights and from the flow of artesian wells capped, or to be capped, lying above the said canal.

In return, the Iowa Syndicate granted all rights-of-way through their described land, 50 feet in width from said canal. The canal would have a sufficient capacity to carry 500 inches and Gage reserved the right to develop and procure water in addition to the 335 inches. If Gage failed to have at least one mile of canal completed by January 1, 1887, the contract would be void. Although the Syndicate agreed to bear its proportion of running expenses of the canal, they would not contribute to enlarging or cementing it.

The Iowa Syndicate's total payment of $167,500 was distributed in installments. The immediate pay-out to Gage of $87,500 helped with his option fee and allowed him to begin his canal.

> The remaining $80,000 will be distributed in installments of $20,000 each upon completion of the canal to the south line of Section 5, and delivery of 335 inches of water, together with a good title, and free from all encumbrances to said water. When the canal is completed to the south line of Section 19, the final payment of $20,000 will transpire.[9]

A full and correct copy of the signed agreement was recorded in San Bernardino Recorder's Office and in Des Moines, Iowa, on August 27, 1885, and legally bonded heirs and assignees of the respected parties.

When Matthew Gage and A. J. Twogood returned to Riverside, there was great speculation about Gage's canal. The *Riverside Press & Horticulturist* announced:

> The great problem of irrigating the dry plains is being solved, and to Mr. Gage more than any other man is due the credit of solving that problem. A number of attempts have been made to irrigate this land by men who have had abundant means but while they were talking, Mr. Gage has been working.

There was joy in the Fourteenth Street house when the family was reunited. When Jane and the children returned from Laguna Beach, they had much news to share with Matthew. Jane disclosed that Frank and Hattie Green, their former landlords, had lost their one-month-old son and she had written condolences from the family. They discussed the new railroad from Riverside to Los Angeles, incorporated as the *Riverside, Santa Ana, & Los Angeles Railroad* to link San Bernardino, Riverside and Los Angeles. Tracks from the Riverside depot on Seventh Street to Arlington would soon be installed directly east of their home, My Sweet Anna.

The children were excited about their father's big project and everyone in town shared opinions about the success of the future canal. Matthew wrote letters to his mother and relatives in Canada, recounting events that were making his gigantic project possible. Roe's Drug Store was filled with customers contemplating the impact of such an extensive canal and what it would do for the community.

Matthew Gage estimated his expenses would amount to $65,000 for construction of the canal, $110,000 to cement it, and $37,000 to perfect title to his water rights and land.[10] Additional water users supplemented his income from mortgages on their property. He continued to contact property owners with land below his proposed canal. His greatest selling point in furnishing water included the provision that water users would become stockholders of the company to be organized upon completion of the canal.

He mortgaged his Riverside property, including his Magnolia Avenue ranch, his family home, and his downtown business building. Bank loans were forthcoming from the Riverside Banking Company, headed by Otis T. Dyer. Alfred Woodill encouraged his friend, loaned him money, and kept informed on each phase of the operation.[11] Matthew announced work would begin on October 1st.

He expected water to be delivered along the entire length to Section 30 by January 1886, an approximate date suggested by his engineers. Because he had under-estimated the complexities of constructing such an irrigation canal, many unexpected problems materialized that delayed progress. Matthew inspected each step of construction and quietly questioned the frequent route changes that seemed unnecessary. He infrequently released short, concise bulletins to local newspapers announcing completion of certain phases, but seldom revealed any details. Townspeople thought he feared some unknown jinx might terminate his enterprise and he therefore remained secretive of the canal's progress.

After three years of unpleasant negotiations, irrigation water became available to Riverside Water Company stockholders for their orchards and vineyards. A zanjero, or water-master, controlled the systematic distribution of water, a similar system used by the Chaffey brothers in their development of Ontario. The Chaffeys, often in the news, made headlines when they installed a small generator near their Etiwanda canal and conveyed a small current to an arc light, an early form of a hydrologic generator.[12]

Matthew signed a contract with S & T Townsend of Los Angeles to dig the U-shaped canal, six feet wide and four feet deep. Construction required exacting measurements for a gravity flow of three feet to a mile over an extended distance to the Tequesquite Arroyo. With a capacity to carry 1,500 inches of water, it was necessary to build four long flumes and blast four formidable tunnels through hard rock. W. H. Perry signed the contract to furnish lumber for the flumes and walls of the tunnels. William Manson, an expert well-borer from Ottawa, Canada, was hired to locate new water sources, sink wells, and discretely cap them for future use.[13] Excavation of Matthew Gage's long-awaited canal began October 7, 1885, as a crew of workers began digging a four-foot wide ditch starting southeast of San Bernardino and half-a-mile above the existing Riverside Water Company canal.

Matthew had many serious concerns pertaining to construction of his canal. However, acquisition of a huge labor force remained the responsibility of the contractor. The Los Angeles firm secured several hundred Chinese men, supervised their work, and paid them regularly in cash. The S & T Company recruited workers through a contract agent representing San Francisco's Six Companies. Chinese laborers paid the association a fee for obtaining work and contributed a percentage of their wages to reduce indenture contracts. Once a week, skilled workers were paid $7.50 and common labors $6.25.[14]

A crew of 20 men began digging a crevice into the hard, dry ground as a Chinese mule-skinner followed with his deep, bladed scraper. Survey stakes defined the canal route as workers picked and shoveled a line across the dry mesa.

Matthew Gage's canal construction was one of three projects taking place east of town at the same time. *The Riverside, Santa Ana & Los Angeles Railroad* had a crew of a hundred workmen laying tracks for their new line. Farther west, another crew worked to improve the Riverside Water Company Canal.[15] At the end of each day, as work progressed along these three individual projects, workmen moved their encampments further south. Wagons, chuck wagons, lumber, and mule teams advanced producing the illusion of a major military operation.

In November 1885, J. Alfonso Carit and a San Bernardino Times reporter paid a visit to Carit's former tract to inspect the progress of Matthew's canal. Three miles of open canal work had been completed and the men were impressed with the use of such modern equipment. The newspaper man reported:

> A number of wells are being sunk, with one well at a depth of 101 feet already flowing 26 inches. Pipe cut into artesian streams produce an enormous flow. Wells are seven-inches in diameter and can be sunk by means of steam well-boring equipment at a rate of 50 feet per day. This machine is the invention of William Manson and is worked by a power engine with two hydraulic jacks that exert a powerful pressure. With this machine a well can be sunk to any depth at about $2.60 per foot.

Manson drilled four more wells during the month, one at 100 feet with 25 inches, one at 125 feet with 50 inches, and two smaller ones. He figured he could dig two to three wells a week with his steam powered hydraulic jack. Each well was capped for future use without diminishing the water supply of other wells.[16]

After Matthew completed his canal, he confessed he had used a water witch to locate underground water.

> I employed a man of local fame called a "water witch." Hidden currents of water in the artesian belt could be located by means of a willow bough and a person of strong, electrical forces. My man drove down stakes and we bore to a depth of 200 feet when we struck a flow of 100 inches to each well. I believe that a current of electricity follows a subterraneous flow of water and the direct locating can be determined by a willow bough and a person endowed with electricity.[17]

Matthew had accumulated a vast supply of water, more than Section 30 required and more than his contractual landowners below the canal could use. In December 1885 Albert S. White paid Matthew $9,000 to supply water for 90 acres that he planned to subdivide near the new Riverside, Santa Ana & Los Angeles train station. Mr. White planned to sell "desirable" residential lots along Seventh Street, to build a reservoir, and to pipe domestic water to each lot. The following year, a 30-man team constructed a brick reservoir where water flowed through strainers and iron pipes and conveyed pure water to each lot of White's Addition.

Riverside Heights Water Company incorporated in order to furnish domestic water from the Gage Canal to White's Addition, and other contiguous properties. Later, this water company contracted to furnish water to Castleman's Addition, a subdivision of John S. Castleman of Kingston, Canada, whose 560 acres was located near Section 30, between Comer and Chicago avenues.[18] Matthew Gage was promising and selling water before a drop ever entered his canal. Astute businessmen questioned the practice of paying for a product that might never be received, stimulating questions as to Matthew's business sense. Nevertheless, Matthew maintained a positive attitude, determined to complete his canal and claim Section 30.

On Christmas Day, Alice Miller and Frank W. Richardson were married in the presence of her family at the Glenwood Hotel. The building, no longer a cottage, had become a hotel with the addition of 20 rooms following Frank Miller's failure to sell the property. During the prosperous boom years of the 1880s, the Glenwood gained a national reputation as a pleasant health resort located in the beautiful city of Riverside, home of the delicious navel orange. Colorful railroad posters publicized that a comfortable living could be realized from the profits of owning a citrus grove and effectively advertised southern California as a latter day Garden of Eden. Reduced fares enticed scores of easterners to come west, especially during the winter months and railroads instigated special excursions and sight-seeing tours.

At the end of the year Samuel Merrill and his family arrived in Colton on a Siegler Winter Excursion. Merrill came to inspect the progress of Gage's canal. The Syndicate's agreement stipulated, "If the party of the first part fails to have at least one mile of said canal completed by January 1, 1886, the contract shall be void with no binding whatever at the option of party of the second part."

On New Year's Day, 1886, Matthew Gage escorted Samuel Merrill on an inspection tour of his canal and the Iowa Syndicate land. It was 65 degrees and cold due to a sharp north wind. As the buggy headed across the mesa, he drove to a water intake along the Santa Ana River and slowly followed an open ditch until it reached the Syndicate's land. The dirt trench extended three miles and, even though gophers and ground squirrels had undermined short sections, Merrill was satisfied that Gage had met his obligation.

Gage Canal

As the two men conversed, Matthew explained that he had several hundred feet of tunnel work to complete, flumes to build, and more open canal work to finish. He proposed cementing the tunnels while the crews were on hand instead of waiting until water was delivered. Cementing tunnels, an expensive operation, was estimated to cost $15,000. Matthew anticipated water would be delivered to the Syndicate's land by March, in time for spring planting.

Samuel Merrill and Matthew Gage recalled their previous inspection trip when they became stuck in the Santa Ana River. Matthew had taken his guest to view his artesian wells and, as they crossed the unusually high river, his horse became stuck in quicksand and went down. Matthew had jumped from the buggy and unhitched his horse as water continued to rise in the buggy containing Samuel Merrill. Matthew floated a nearby log to the buggy, forming a pontoon bridge for Merrill to reach the bank and safe ground. The men now laughed at the thought of too much water, after years of searching for any water at all.[19] Now, winter rains filled the river again. Runoff from the mountains entered Mill Creek and rains off Old Baldy added to the heavy volume of the river.

In order to promote sales of southern California oranges, Riverside growers participated in the 1886 Chicago Citrus Fair and filled five boxcars with local citrus. Riverside's patriotic display with dishes of colorful fruit arranged in pyramids, garnished with small American flags, gained national attention. Plates of raisins and fancy oranges were displayed with signs "Grown in Riverside, California" associating desirable navel oranges with the southern California town.

Matthew Gage had many problems in 1886, with the first major one occurring on January 23. Three Riverside men filed affidavits of contest against him alleging that he had not reclaimed any part of Section 30. These entry men, William Edward Atwater, Johannis Jacob Gunther, and (Hjalmer) Otto Newman, claimed that Gage had not applied water onto Section 30 within the three year period from date of his entry.

The men hired an attorney to search land records and were informed that the property was open to contest and that Gage's Desert Land entry was subject to cancellation. Furthermore, their attorney believed that the land had not been reclaimed according to "the spirit and tenor of the Desert Act." Consequently, each man applied for a Homestead and Timber Culture entry to portions of quarter sections in Section 30.

The first Homestead application filed on January 23, 1886, in the Los Angeles Land Office was numbered 6795 and read:

> I, William Edward Atwater, of Riverside, San Bernardino County, California, do hereby apply to enter under section 2289, revised Statues of the United States, the Lot 1 and NE 1/4 of M W/, and N fi of N E /of Section 30 in Township No. 2, South of Range No. 4, West of San Bernardino Meridian, Containing 159.28 acres.
> W. H. Seamans, Register of Land Office.[20]

To make matters worse for Matthew, other people were also claiming ownership rights to Section 30. Austin and Keeney of Riverside had filed a claim prior to Atwater, Gunther, and Newman. A man named Swanwick, a well known irrigator living near the Tequesquite Arroyo, had moved his house onto Section 30 where he subsequently lived undisturbed for several years. His shack stood near the southeast corner, above the canal route where gravity flow could not reach and consequently, no one paid attention to Mr. Swanwick.

Matthew appealed to the United States Land Department in Los Angeles requesting additional time to apply water to his claim. He presented proof of his efforts, introducing C. C. Miller's water measurements, and inferred the canal would be completed within months. The sympathetic judge took into consideration the difficult circumstances that Gage had encountered in constructing the canal and issued a temporary patent. The claim jumpers did not give up their quest, however. Forty-one-year-old Matthew Gage had a perplexing, complicated year ahead as he attempted to complete his canal plagued with continuous construction problems and legal consequences from three men determined to take Section 30.

CHAPTER 4

On New Year's Day, 1886, a deluxe, parlor car came to a stop on the tracks of a railroad spur near Fourteenth and Mulberry streets. The new *Riverside, Santa Ana & Los Angeles Railroad* had been completed from San Bernardino to Casa Blanca, where a new depot had been built near Henry Lockwood's house on Magnolia Avenue. Matthew, Jane, and the children hurried to the railroad car to greet their Canadian relatives who had come to spend the winter. Matthew's brother, Robert, Robert's wife, Mary (Irving), their children, and his mother, Margaret Jane Orr Gage, were cheerfully escorted across the street to My Sweet Anna. Matthew had summoned his brother to assist in completing the canal.

Matthew's 76-year-old mother had been a widow for three decades and her sons and daughters doted on her every whim. Jane was fond of her charming mother-in-law and the children, intrigued with their imposing grandmother, eagerly introduced her to their pet dogs, King and Queenie. They were anxious to show off their flourishing orange trees, heavy with clusters of ripe fruit ready to enjoy. Matthew provided his relatives with comfortable lodgings and the Gage family rejoiced at being together under one roof again. Two days later, on January 3, the temperature

Margaret Jane Orr Gage

dropped to nearly 20 degrees and the Canadian visitors wondered if they were truly in sunny California.

Some time earlier, Frank Miller had sold his Blue Front Grocery Store to a pleasant man named E. C. Love, who at the beginning of the year began a "cash only" business. Matthew entered the store a few days later and asked Mr. Love if he could borrow five dollars. The friendly grocer did not hesitate and handed Matthew a five dollar gold piece and asked if he was in need of more. Matthew thanked him and said it was enough to buy a few groceries. As Mr. Love filled Matthew's order, he questioned the wisdom of his new "cash only business." Matthew purchased his groceries with money he had borrowed from the storekeeper and left the store smiling. People next door in the drug store had a good laugh at Matthew Gage's droll Irish humor.[1]

Matthew traveled frequently to San Francisco where he had established a line of credit with several banks and insurance companies. Several of these contacts were perhaps due to his association with J. Alfonso Carit. In 1883, he had befriended Carit, his wife Francisa and their three children, when they lived in San Bernardino and remained on friendly terms with the family. Carit attempted to follow the progress of Gage's canal through correspondence with former southern California neighbors.

As completion of his remarkable canal became imminent, Matthew Gage found himself a celebrity. California newspapers ran admiring stories about his astounding foresight in pursuing such a mammoth project. Not all of the publicity was complimentary however. He continued to be noncommittal about details of his project causing an atmosphere of skepticism concerning the canal and the man. A San Bernardino reporter wrote:

> Riverside's greatest object is to get water and her continued growth demands more and more. The value of water has grown so that an inch is worth a fabulous sum delivered. The Gage wells are an experiment,

a costly one to the property owners in the vicinity. The Riverside Water Company is proposing sinking another group of wells that will drain this place, as the Gage wells have done. San Bernardino is situated immediately above a subterranean lake that is supplied from rainfall on the surrounding mountains and from this we get our artesian water. With Riverside, and Gage taking our water, San Bernardino will be drained and ruined.[2]

Nevertheless, many people in town thought highly of Matthew Gage and a movement unfolded to name a new street in his honor. It was suggested that Grand Gage Boulevard, a duplication of tree-lined Magnolia Avenue, be located east of town near the Gage Canal.[3] For unknown reasons the street never materialized, but years later a two-lane road named Iowa Avenue extended across Iowa Syndicate's land. In April, 1886, the *Los Angeles Times* reported:

The title of Matthew Gage's water tract has been perfected. The supply consists of the oldest established water rights on the Santa Ana River for a distance of three miles, from its commencement of use and artesian wells. The canal can carry 3,500 inches, a sufficient volume to irrigate 10,000 acres of land. Mr. Gage is to be congratulated for having brought to conclusion such a successful and important irrigating enterprise yet inaugurated in southern California.

Tourist companies predicted Riverside would become even more of a paradise with the completion of the Gage Canal.[4] Real estate promoters traveled from town to town, eagerly searching for lucrative land bargains. Real estate in southern California was booming, mainly due to railroad advertising and reduced fares to solicit business. Rate wars between competing railroads further lowered ticket prices. One day the fare from Kansas City to Riverside dropped to

$25 and another day the fare from Boston to Riverside was only $25. In March 1886, special first class tickets from Boston to California cost one dollar.

The grand opening of the *Riverside, Santa Ana & Los Angeles Railroad* became a great convenience for travelers with four connections a day to San Diego, Los Angeles, and eastern destinations. In the months ahead, local citizens grew unhappy about having railroad tracks bisecting their town and dismayed that the City had given the company right-of-way to use and cross any street.

Southern California, with its excellent weather and an abundance of garden and fruit bearing trees, became a paradise for tramps and hobos. Train tracks offered inviting, easy roadways as this transit population traveled town to town, consuming whatever was available. The situation became serious and Riverside fruit growers deemed it necessary to take the law into their own hands. A vigilante committee organized to stop brazen stealing of oranges and the depletion of their crops. Written warnings were posted all over town notifying tramps to leave Riverside before 8:30 at night or the newly organized vigilante committee would deal with them.[5] Matthew Gage, and his neighbors, posted signs on their fences and kept their dogs outside on long tethers.

Even though the future appeared bright and encouraging, Matthew Gage was spending sums that he didn't have and was subsequently forced to borrow $100,000 from his friend, Adoniram J. Twogood. He received the money in United States gold coin in exchange for his promissory note, agreeing to repay by September 1st plus interest, "according to the terms of two other promissory notes."[6] Matthew prophesized delivery of water onto Section 30 would be worth substantially more than all his debts. Regardless of his indebtedness, Matthew had another idea, a secret plan whereby he could substantially increase his financial worth.

In July, Robert Gage escorted his mother, his wife and his children back to Canada for the summer. They had spent a delightful winter in Riverside and, as the summer

Artesian Wells on the Gage Canal

heat approached, they had decided to return to their homes in Kingston. After getting his family settled, Robert returned to Riverside to supervise the continuing construction of additional redwood plank flumes for the Gage Canal. He had become his brother's right-hand man, offering engineering and architectural advice concerning four vital canal flumes.

In July 1886, the San Bernardino County assessment rates were set at $1.50 per $100 valuation. The value of land under the Gage Canal had increased to $25 an acre, a substantial increase from the 1885 valuation of $1 an acre.[7] There were some 6,000 acres with an assessed valuation of $150,000 as opposed to the year before at $1 an acre totaling $6,000. The value of land significantly increased in anticipation of the delivery of water, even though not a drop had yet entered the canal.

Matthew was no longer secretive about the construction of his canal and allowed frequent interviews, encounters that he seemingly enjoyed. *Riverside's Press & Horticulturist* printed the following personal story that the Gage family preserved:

About two years ago Matthew Gage undertook to solve the problem of watering the dry plain. He proceeded to develop his plan for irrigating and plastered his property pretty well over with mortgages having confidence in the future of this country and the advance in the price of real estate. When Mr. Gage commenced his work, no one thought he would succeed. Citizens were very slow to learn that Matthew Gage supervised all the work and remained its sole owner and proprietor. With his method of attending artesian wells, he was revolutionizing the irrigation systems to a great extent.[8]

Many of Matthew Gage's friends still deemed it a visionary scheme to convey water such a great distance and questioned his ability and expertise. Few people believed a former jeweler, of modest means, could undertake and achieve such a mammoth project alone. Citizens questioned who was backing Gage and who truly was building the canal. Water users near San Bernardino who also utilized water from Mill Creek, Warm Creek, and Spring Brook were resentful. When water became scarce, Riverside and Matthew Gage were blamed for taking their supply. In retaliation dams, ditches, and flumes were occasionally damaged or destroyed and water rights were openly challenged.

In order to protect his essential headwaters in the Santa Ana River, Matthew had a large, two-story frame house constructed on his 540 acre tract containing valuable artesian wells. In the summer of 1885, he had hired William Manson, an expert well-digger from Canada, and placed him and his family in the new house. Manson continued searching for additional water sources and guarded the property containing valuable capped wells. The value of Gage's wells was estimated to be more than $250,000.

William Manson improved the 40 acres surrounding his house, creating a beautifully landscaped park with shade trees, fountains, and lawns. The extraordinary retreat, named Victoria Tract in honor of Queen Victoria, became a favorite outing for church and school picnics.[9] Not everyone living in San Bernardino appreciated Matthew's generous gesture of using San Bernardino's water to establish a free park for the enjoyment of Riversiders.

While Matthew continued to supervise his canal project, his family escaped the hot summer and vacationed in Del Mar with its magnificent beach. Small summer cottages stood along the sloping hillsides near the picturesque hotel overlooking the ocean. Jane and the children stayed at Mr. J. S. Taylor's hotel, a fashionable resort, frequented by Riverside families. One of the hotel's attractions included an unusual pool that filled with sea water during high tide. The Gage children, Margaret, 16, Maude, 10, Horace, 6, and Robert, 3, enjoyed their ocean swim without an undertow or frightening waves.

By August, the canal was advancing towards the Point of Rocks, a rocky knoll that presented serious problems. Two crews, one at either end of a solid rock mound, began chipping through the hard earth. It proved to be the longest, most difficult undertaking in the entire system. Workers drilled at both ends and slowly worked with picks and axes to carve out a path through the solid granite. Teams of strong men worked night and day, in the heat of summer, to complete the 1,040-foot tunnel. Finally, at 3 o'clock in the morning on August 21, the two crews cut through the final ledge and connected. Christopher Columbus Miller received much credit for the accuracy of his calculations. It was a happy day when daylight streamed through the entire tunnel, even though it had been an expensive endeavor at $8 a foot.[10]

In the fall, Iowan Stephen Herrick moved to Riverside with his family where he could observe Matthew Gage's progress and supervise the Iowa Syndicate's interests. Mr. Herrick and A. J. Twogood became partners in a real estate business. In order to develop their 2,000-acre investment, the Iowa Company incorporated as the East Riverside Land Company and the East Riverside Water Company, with water and canal rights in the Gage Canal. In time, an agricultural community developed in the area, first named Merrill, and later Highgrove.

Matthew was endeavoring to complete his canal when William and George Chaffey sold their Etiwanda and Ontario subdivisions and began a new venture in Australia. They were invited to develop a 250,000-acre colony, utilizing water and land principles that they had used in southern California. After several years of dealing with agricultural problems and foreign ownership laws, George returned to California while his brother remained in Australia.[11]

During the fall, Matthew became convinced that he had more than enough water to reclaim Section 30. Well-digger Manson continued discovering good flowing wells every week. Ever optimistic, Matthew commenced purchasing useless, dry land on the south side of Tequesquite Arroyo. In October 1886, he bought 1,400 acres from Isabell Russell for $69,829.[12] The following week he contracted with Samuel C. Evans and the Riverside Land & Irrigating Company to purchase 1,600 acres, at $75 an acre, with payment due as land sold.[13] He had decided to extend his irrigation canal, on grade, approximately nine miles to the range of hills near the

Riverside Banking Company. Corner of Ninth and Main Streets.

Temescal Tin Mine property. A long, sturdy, flume across the big arroyo would be necessary to convey water to some 5,000 dry, unproductive acres.

When news of Matthew's latest undertaking circulated around town, some citizens questioned his wisdom and credibility. He had not applied one drop of water to land owners who were still awaiting completion of his auspicious irrigating canal. How could he commit water to distant places when many people in his original service area had been waiting for several years?

Unperturbed by gossip, Matthew pursued his dream of developing the land south of the arroyo into countless, beautiful citrus groves and hired C.C. Miller to survey the barren land. Local leaders optimistically calculated the Gage Canal, and other irrigating systems, would eventually support a population of 50,000 citizens.

Real estate sales continued to escalate with hundreds of tourists visiting southern California. New residents informed hometown friends and relatives of the perfect climate and beautiful countryside. The boom of the 1880s was at its height during 1886 and 1887 with exaggerated newspaper articles adding to the frenzy of the times. Newcomers were introduced to the delicious, seedless navel orange and Riverside soon appeared on maps.

During the first week of November 1886, Matthew announced water would be turned on in his canal. It was postponed, however, due to unfinished work in one of the difficult tunnels. He announced to land owners holding notes or mortgages for water delivery they would not be required to pay interest until water was actually received.

With no prior announcement, a small head of water flowed into the canal on Tuesday, November 9, at 2 o'clock in the afternoon. Jane Gage, assisted by her children, had the honor of raising the head-gate, allowing water to enter the dirt lined channel.[14] Matthew and a crew of workmen, watched water slowly trickle along the open canal. Workmen removed debris and tumbleweeds from the open trough as water slowly advanced. Several Chinese men patched holes and cracks in the dirt canal as gophers and squirrels scurried away. A small stream of water continued slowly through the canal, inching along all day and all night.

The next morning, Stephen Herrick drove to the Iowa Syndicate's land where he observed men pitching tumbleweeds from the canal. Other buggies soon arrived as word spread through town that water was in Gage's canal. As water progressed towards the Syndicate's property, Stephen Herrick grabbed a shovel and went to work. He dug an opening to each 10-acre parcel, allowing water onto the land. He was well-versed on the Satterwaite Act of 1876 that "guaranteed a water right on land that had once been irrigated by a water company, thereby making its easement perpetual."[15]

At sunset on November 10th, water finally reached Section 30. In later years, testimony revealed that little, if any, water dampened Gage's land as the canal skirted a shallow arroyo where the water ceased flowing, leaving the southeastern corner dry. Due to lack of water, or the darkness of night, the water terminus remained questionable. Matthew had obtained easements to a bluff over looking the Tequesquite Arroyo where run-off water spilled into the arroyo.

The following day, Matthew turned the water off at the head-gates, claiming that customers were not ready for delivery. Stephen Herrick presented Matthew Gage a final check for $67,500 that was deposited in the Riverside Banking Company to credit his account. O. T. Dyer, president of the bank, became the temporary financial manager of the Gage Canal. The Iowa Syndicate received the first 335 inches of water in the new canal, free and clear of all encumbrances.

Matthew Gage became the man of the hour. He was hailed a courageous hero as congratulations complimented his persistent work and ability to overcome enormous obstacles. The completion of his successful canal became important news and articles about his outstanding achievements appeared in Los Angeles, San Diego, and San Francisco newspapers. His brother, Robert, received credit for his innovative engineering skills, especially for the construction of the complex flumes. *The San Diego Sun* reflected upon Matthew's attributes and quoted: "It is the borrower, not the capitalist, as a rule who is the greatest benefit to a community."

Before water entered the canal on November 9th, Matthew had signed contracts with several property owners south of the Tequesquite Arroyo agreeing to supply water to their dry lands. C.O. Perrine was his first customer to request connections south of the arroyo. He proposed developing a new cemetery on his Mount Pachappa property that housed his industrial brickyard and kiln.[16] Riverside's original cemetery, at the base of Mount Rubidoux, remained covered in weeds.

Another customer south of the arroyo was Priestley Hall, owner of Hall's Addition to Riverside consisting of a 280-acre tract. He planned to develop his land with water from the Gage Canal, but did not subscribe for delivery until 1888. He had worked for C. C. Miller in surveying the Gage Canal and admired Matthew Gage's conscientious initiative. In June 1887, he incorporated Hall's Addition Street Railroad Company and was granted a city franchise for a line from Tenth and Main streets to Date Street. It consisted of a single track, one car, and four mules.

After the first flow of water passed through the canal, a group of squatters invaded Section 30. William Edward Atwater, Otto Newman, and Jacob Gunter filed individual Homestead affidavits, documents claiming the land,

Priestly Hall

63

certified by the Commissioner of General Land Office.[17] Their petitions stated that Gage had not applied the required water within the specified three years, and their attorney reported "the land open for settlement." Atwater was familiar with the property, having walked across it since 1882 on his way to hunt in the Box Springs Mountains. As the ringleader, he was determined Matthew Gage had not fulfilled requirements of the Desert Land Act to reclaim Section 30. This unexpected turn of events initiating 19 years of frustrations, censures and questionable judicial proceedings, complicated the lives of all involved, especially that of Matthew Gage.

A month after water was applied to Section 30, Matthew, Jane, and the children left for Kingston, Canada, to celebrate the Christmas holidays with family members. They visited his mother, Margaret Gage, brothers Robert and John, sisters Eliza Irving and Sarah Spooner. Jane's parents, the Gibsons, were happy to have their daughter and grandchildren for the holidays and were introduced to Anna and Robert who had been born in California. Matthew encouraged everyone to visit or move to Riverside and enjoy a good life and be financially comfortable growing oranges. He explained that real estate was a profitable endeavor, that "people were paying hundreds of dollars an acre for good climate, with a little dirt thrown in."[18]

Two weeks after returning to Riverside, Matthew offered to furnish the City of Riverside piped domestic water from his wells. Townspeople had long been unhappy with unsanitary and unsightly open ditches along downtown streets. City officials attempted to keep the canals clean and fined sheepherders $9 for every animal caught drinking from them. Matthew offered a supply of 200 to 300 inches of pure artesian water, under pressure, piped directly from his wells to City connections. In return, he would take cash or shares in a company to be organized. He asked no money from the City, or the Riverside Land Company, or the Riverside Water Company. He declared pressure in his water pipes would be

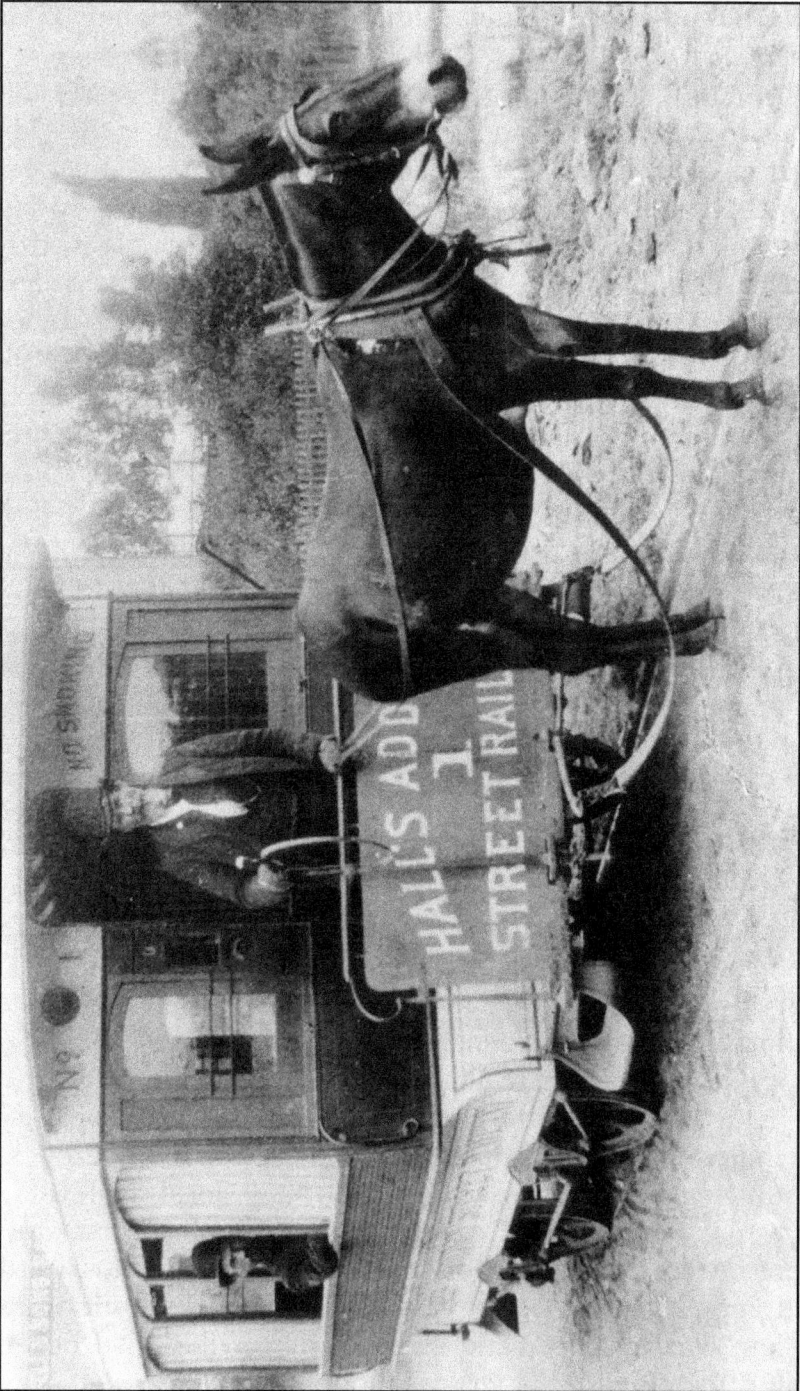

Hall's Addition Street Railway.

65

forceful enough to eliminate the need of fire engines in an emergency.

Emil Rosenthal, a local merchant turned real estate developer, submitted a counter-proposal to the city. His plan involved piping 200 inches of water from the Riverside Water Company's property in San Bernardino to local storage reservoirs. In return, Rosenthal and his backers planned to purchase land around Rubidoux Mountain for $25,000 and develop it into choice home sites. In addition, they planned to build a grand resort hotel, designed in a Swiss Gothic style of architecture, to be named the Rubidoux. The 240 room hotel would be located on the crest of the hill and command a panoramic view.

Deliberations about the two competing proposals continued until February 18, 1887 when directors of the Riverside Water Company board ultimately accepted Rosenthal's proposal. Board members included many of Matthew Gage's Canadian friends, as well as Joseph Jarvis, who had helped organize the water company. John G. North, superintendent of the water company, was instrumental in the board's acceptance of Rosenthal's plan. He favored City ownership over individual ownership. Newspapers reported Gage's offer contained certain advantages over Rosenthal's, in that control of the system would be in the hands of a board of directors whose main interest would be irrigating agricultural land and providing water for domestic use. Under Rosenthal's plan the City would own the pipelines and reap the benefits. Ultimately, many citizens doubted Matthew's ability to supply enough water to all his prospective customers.

Rosenthal's subdivision, Rubidoux Heights, consisted of choice view lots situated along the eastern slope of the mountain. John Jarvis, who had many local real estate investments, purchased several lots and built a three-story mansion for his family on the eastern corner of Twelfth and Pepper (Redwood) streets.[19] A $200,000 domestic water system was installed, and construction of the hotel began. Unfortunately, few investors bought stock in the hotel

John T. Jarvis House 1888

company. Construction on the hotel came to a halt, due to both a violent wind storm that demolished the initial framework of the building and to serious financial problems. The Riverside Banking Company had invested heavily in the hotel project and later became insolvent, with major losses to stockholders and depositors. Rosenthal lost a fortune, declared bankruptcy, and died a broken man.[20]

Matthew turned water into his canal on February 20, 1887 to flow permanently for the benefit of stockholders and to reclaim Section 30. Although the water disappeared into gopher holes and dirt slides, a small amount reached the end of the canal and run-off water spilled into the Tequesquite Arroyo. Agents for the Iowa Syndicate, White's Addition, Castleman's Addition and Matthew Gage all began advertising in newspapers "available land for sale with water." Matthew advertised, "Land to rent in Section 30. Parties willing to put in grain with water from Gage Canal. Contact M. Gage."

In the spring, two out-of-town families registered at the St. George Hotel in downtown Riverside. Members of both families suddenly came down with smallpox, a highly contagious disease. Two children died and remaining family members were quickly isolated. A smallpox epidemic was capable of killing hundreds of Riversiders. Matthew Gage came to the rescue and solved the isolation problem by leasing to the city, free of charge, five acres, in a remote corner of Section 30. City workers moved a simple frame structure onto the site and Matthew furnished free water to the quarantined families. The modest, plain building, known as the Pest House, stood on Section 30 for 12 years.[21]

On March 1, 1887 Matthew's brother, John, and his wife, Mary, arrived in Riverside to become permanent residents. They were each blessed with beautiful singing voices and perfect diction and performed in church functions and drama recitations. John invested in an orange grove on Indiana Avenue and Matthew and Jane were happy to have family living in Riverside.

Sunday services at Magnolia Avenue Presbyterian Church were frequently cancelled after groves surrounding the church had been irrigated. Parishioners did not wish to wade through mud and irrigation water to attend services. Signs were posted announcing "No services as roads are impassable." In 1886, Reverend Henry B. Gage accepted the call to preside at the church. Even though he was not related to the Matthew Gage family, a certain amount of confusion persisted between the two families for some time. In the spring, Matthew and Jane found the long drive to the Magnolia church had become a hardship on the entire family. Jane discovered she was pregnant, for the seventh time, and had no desire to ride over bumpy roads only to discover "no services today."

The Gages invited fellow Presbyterians living near town to join them in the Pavilion on Sundays. Individuals took turns reading from the Bible and small gatherings sang hymns directed by John and Mary Gage. When weather became unpleasant, the small congregation shared their homes where pianos occasionally offered welcome music. On June 4, plans for a new Riverside Episcopal Church were accepted by members and a week later, a new Congregational Church was dedicated at the corner of Seventh and Lemon streets. With other denominations building their houses of worship, downtown Presbyterians acknowledged the time had come to organize their own church.

On June 19, 1887, several devoted church members, led by Matthew Gage, traveled to Los Angeles for the purpose of establishing another Riverside Presbyterian church. The Los Angeles Presbytery authorized a new church and Matthew Gage suggested the name Calvary.[22] The 27 charter members included Mr. and Mrs. Matthew Gage, Margaret Gage, an adult at 17; Matthew's mother, Margaret Gage; his brother Robert Gage; his sister, Mrs. Sarah Spooner; and friends Mrs. Alfred Woodill and Hiram Craft. Reverend J. B. Stewart of Des Moines, Iowa accepted the position of pastor with an annual salary of $2,000. The small congregation met in various donated meeting places until they could build their own church. John and Mary Gage sang at the Sunday services as did a young school girl named Marcia Craft.

During the first summer of the Gage Canal's operation, Matthew faced serious problems when his dams and ditches along the Santa Ana River were mysteriously damaged or destroyed. Officers of the Riverside Water Company were rumored to have cut the dams, allowing water to pass into their own ditches. At the time, there were 200 inches of water flowing into the Gage Canal and there seemed to be a difference of opinion as to the amount to which Gage was entitled. Resentment heightened over Gage's ownership of so much water and his reluctance to relinquish some to the people of Riverside.

John G. North, superintendent, and R. E. Houghton, the company's attorney, challenged Matthew Gage's right to his water intake at a certain point in the river. They were of the opinion he should receive only the amount of water old ditches once carried. Gage, and his San Bernardino attorneys, claimed that he had a right to all water in the river at the head of his canal under a previous equitable purchase. His attorneys obtained warrants for the arrest of all parties connected with destroying Gage's boulder dams and ditches. Matthew hired a retired sheriff to guard his canal intake near the Santa Ana River and the presence of a long barreled rifle eliminated any further damage.[23]

The Riverside Water Company filed suit against Matthew Gage contending that he had diverted and impeded progress of their water flow consisting of 450 miner's inches and asked for $5,000 in damages and costs. The court issued an injunction restraining Matthew from diverting any flow in excess of 330 miner's inches. It also upheld his riparian rights at his canal heading and confirmed his ownership of some 2,300 acres located on both sides of the Santa Ana River.

Newspapers were quick to point out "a law suit would hurt both Riverside and the Gage Canal people, not by loss of water but by the unfriendly talk it will give rise to." Subsequently a ruling limited the Gage Canal to 300 miner's inches from the river during May through September. Matthew instructed William Manson to continue drilling additional wells in his artesian belt and this successful endeavor generously supplemented the amount of water intake limited by the court. Even though the suit was settled in Matthew Gage's favor, hard feelings persisted over his ownership of such a large volume of water. John G. North, R. E. Houghton, and Matthew Gage were destined to tangle again.

In the summer of 1886, an advertisement appeared in local newspapers announcing "20-acres of improved land in Arlington for sale cheap, terms easy. M. Gage P.O. Box 447, Riverside." The Arlington ranch owned jointly by Matthew and Robert Gage was sold. The following year Matthew sold his jewelry store building on Main Street to James Bettner for $12,000.[24] Mr. Bettner, a wealthy New Yorker, also purchased the Blue Front Grocery Store. He had moved to Riverside for his health in 1879 and built a comfortable house on Jefferson Street for his wife and two sons. Matthew disposed of his property to finance construction of a sturdy, long flume across the Tequesquite Arroyo. He planned to extend his canal for nine more miles.

A preliminary survey revealed that the extension of the canal would add 8.2 miles to the original 11.9 miles. With an adequate water supply extending over 20 miles, the canal would be able to irrigate hundreds of acres and make them productive. Matthew figured that he could then sell this extensive acreage for hundreds of thousands of dollars and eliminate all his debts.

That summer Jane was unable to join her friends vacationing in Del Mar. On September 13, she gave birth to baby Frances Gibson. The family now consisted of Matthew, Jane, Margaret, Maude, Horace, Robert, Anna, Frances and two happy dogs. It was a busy household where everyone had assigned chores and the family always found time for Bible study and daily prayers. The Gages embraced good literature, fine music and appreciation of Scriptures.

In the fall, Matthew was ready to build the huge flume across the Tequesquite Arroyo, estimating that it would take 90 days to complete. The proposed nine-mile canal south of the arroyo would supply one inch of water to every five acres of land under a four-inch pressure. Water from the main canal would be delivered in iron pipes to each 10-acre parcel.

Matthew named this extensive area, south of the Tequesquite Arroyo, Arlington Heights, due to its slightly elevated location overlooking the town of Arlington.[25] Arlington Heights and the community of Arlington were within the city limits of Riverside, then encompassing 56 square miles. Arlington Heights promised to be the most desirable residential and agricultural land in all of southern California.

The approaching winter of 1887 was predicted to be the busiest tourist season ever experienced in southern California. Booming towns relied on aggressive advertising campaigns as each maneuvered to attract the greatest number of excursionists. Los Angeles real estate promoters spread word that Riverside had ten cases of smallpox in an attempt to deter potential buyers from looking elsewhere. Nevertheless, a tide of tourists headed for Riverside, and Matthew Gage was ready to sell his 10,000 acres.

CHAPTER 5

The 1888 navel orange crop promised to be excellent with an abundance of good-sized, flavorful fruit. Cold nights added to the growth of the oranges, but the chill factor also put growers on guard whenever thermometers dipped below 30 degrees. Many were prepared to flood their orchards, or to use smudge pots to raise temperatures and prevent fruit damage from frost. The year also began with a multitude of complaints over the disappearance of orange crops. Thieving in orange groves had become a major crime in Riverside and it appeared that the culprits knew what they were doing. They were wise in their choice of fruit, only picking good oranges with the aid of special citrus pruning clippers. Respectable tourists were occasionally guilty of pilfering, but generally claimed they had received permission from hotel proprietors or livery men. A polished gentleman and two ladies were caught filling a wagon with choice fruit without permission from the property owner. Sacks of picked oranges were often hidden in a grove to be retrieved at a later date or after dark. Loss of a once-a-year crop became a devastating hardship to any horticulturist.

Matthew had John guard the grove adjacent to My Sweet Anna. January had been a wet month and, fortunately for citrus growers, wagons loaded with oranges could not maneuver through mud. The crop remained on the trees until legitimate pickers were hired. Matthew's attention, however, focused on providing water to the vast acreage south of the big arroyo.

In order to deliver a sufficient water supply to thousands of acres south of his existing canal, Matthew had to build a long flume across the deep Tequesquite Arroyo. Wooden trestles, supporting flumes across arroyos or canyons, had become a common sight in California since the early gold rush days. In February 1888, Matthew hired the Grant Brothers of

Flume Across Tequesquite Arroyo to Arlington Heights   1888

Los Angeles to build a trestle-flume for $6,000.[1] His brother
Robert, living in Riverside, drew the intricate plans, allowing
for separate horizontal sections to be replaced when necessary.
With completion of the flume, the canal would be extended to
John and McAlister streets.

Strong pine and redwood supports were constructed
16 feet apart, rising from cement foundations. The 1,000-foot-
long structure stood 90 feet high, at its tallest point, and
stretched across the arroyo with a precise fall to ensure a
proper gravity flow. In order to save lumber and money, a
section of trestle was built atop a slight knoll and then took
a sharp directional turn to reach the south side of the arroyo.
Floors and side walls of the canal were coated with a thick
mixture of tar and asphalt to seal the wood and eliminate
seepage.

Evenly spaced, short wooden slats were placed across
the top of the flume for the use of "canal walkers." This
dangerous maneuver was a balancing act for skilled men who
regularly inspected and made necessary repairs. Daredevil
youths occasionally challenged each other to walk across the

narrow slats, high above the big arroyo and, unfortunately, more than one young boy fell to his death. Spectators gathered daily to observe construction of the high and long trestle. One day, however, construction was halted as the Tequesquite Arroyo filled with water from a seven inch rain within 24 hours.

Nevertheless, the big arroyo flume was completed within 90 days, a remarkable engineering achievement. On March 31, 1888, Matthew's mother, Margaret Jane Gage, raised the water head-gate, located on the north bluff of the Tequesquite Arroyo, allowing water to seep into the extended canal and flow onto Arlington Heights. The official opening of Arlington Heights was a memorable day and a valuable addition to the city of Riverside. Matthew Gage considered the extension of his canal, and the fortune it would generate, as the ultimate solution to his increasing financial troubles.

There was little celebration in the Gage household, however, for their dear friend Alfred H. Woodill had died the previous day. He had been ill for several weeks and local newspapers issued daily bulletins as to his welfare. Matthew visited him daily and appreciated his interest in the progress of the Tequesquite trestle. Water had been delivered onto Arlington Heights two days before he died and Matthew believed his closest friend had forestalled death long enough to witness the accomplishment. Alfred Woodill had been his greatest advocate in building the canal, both with encouragement and financial aid.[2]

Dr. Woodill's funeral was held at 3 o'clock, April 7, 1888, in his Twelfth Street home where the Masons, the Odd Fellows, and the Knights of Pythias conducted services. Many of his devoted patients remembered his kind acts during their trying times of illness. At the conclusion of the funeral services, his wife and son led those present in walking behind the casket as it was carried ceremoniously to Evergreen Cemetery and buried. Matthew had lost his staunchest supporter and best friend.[3]

In June 1888, the extension of the canal added 8.2 miles to the original 11.9 miles, making the Gage Canal more than 20-miles long. With available water delivered to Arlington Heights, Matthew envisioned the entire area covered in flourishing citrus groves and handsome homes. He had improved the tract with water and now hoped to sell parcels to prospective citrus growers at a respectable profit. Newly planted citrus groves were averaging $500 to $800 an acre.

Matthew sent word to his brother-in-law, William Irving, requesting his help. Irving, married to his sister Eliza, had many years of experience as a civil engineer in Kingston, Canada. Matthew requested his expertise in surveying thousands of acres of barren land, in determining suitable streets and roads and in developing a grand boulevard through the entire area. Visitors to Riverside continued to admire tree-lined Magnolia Avenue and Matthew desired a similar, divided road through his property.

Canada experienced a long, cold winter in 1888, and Eliza and William Irving were anxious to visit southern California. The Irving family made arrangements for an extended visit with the possibility of a permanent move.

My Sweet Anna, Gage House Addition   1888

Before their arrival, Matthew ordered 30,000 navel orange trees from the Twogood Nursery, to be planted in Arlington Heights. A. J. Twogood and D. C. Twogood owned a nursery specializing in budded navel orange trees and were pleased to deal with Matthew, anticipating larger orders in the future.

A. J. Twogood decided to build a house on his profitable orange grove property located on the southwest corner of Mulberry and Fourteenth streets near My Sweet Anna. Architect-builder A. W. Boggs completed the $5,500 two-story, ten-room house in the summer of 1888. It was quite elaborate, with a conical corner tower topped by a metal weathervane. Beautiful stained-glass scenes depicting birds and flowers were installed in polished wood doors and windows. Rooms downstairs opened into one another with sliding doors, producing one grand room, ideal for group gatherings. A large two-story barn and stable stood behind the house where oranges were occasionally packed for shipment to Iowa friends. A. J. Twogood earned $6,500 that year from his six acres of navel oranges, more than the cost of his elaborate house.[4] Matthew and Jane were pleased to have such good neighbors and the families became close friends.

With the influx of tourists seeking bargain land prices, real estate values often doubled and tripled within a short period. Shrewd speculators and businessmen frequently turned over the same property within the same day. Adding to the frenzy of potential buyers, and the dreams of easy money, William Spaulding's popular, one dollar book described "how to grow oranges and achieve a healthy, prosperous future."

It illustrated proper patterns for planting citrus nursery stock and empathized the importance of regular, scheduled furrow irrigation. It explained that trunks of young trees should be wrapped to prevent sunburn and rodent damage. It listed several popular citrus varieties, including the Riverside navel orange, described as highly desirable with its smooth skin, absence of seeds, and sweet flavor. The author concluded: "Orange culture affords a person both a career and revenue."[5]

Riverside had attracted a number of prestigious residents such as Priestley Hall, John Jarvis, and Stephen Herrick. Each had built impressive homes for their families and become active citrus growers. The expanding town was attracting a new wave of industrious, devoutly Christian, community-spirited transplants.

In the spring of 1888, a wooden pole was placed at the corner of Seventh and Main Streets where city officials installed an experimental electric arc light. After dark it was activated as people gathered to view the latest innovation in their city. Matthew and Jane joined the crowd as they watched the light flicker and dance. A distant, humming noise could be heard from a newly installed generator, three miles away near Highgrove. The Riverside Water Canal had installed a 40-foot water drop activating a generator that produced electricity for the arc light.[6] Matthew recalled that the Chaffeys had produced the first electricity in southern California several years earlier by use of Etiwanda Colony irrigation water to operate a small generator.

In the summer, Matthew had a $1,000 addition built onto his Fourteenth Street house. Contractor J. E. Porter completed a new wing, including several upstairs bedrooms and sleeping porches and a new parlor and enlarged dining room downstairs. Electric light poles had been installed along Fourteenth Street and the family made provisions to receive electricity. Matthew noted "these are modern times as kerosene succeeded the tallow dip and gas succeeded kerosene, so is electricity succeeding gas."

Matthew began a search for suitable house rentals to accommodate his visiting Canadian relatives who were arriving in the fall. Robert's family included his wife, three daughters and two sons. His sister, Eliza Gage Irving, and her husband, William, had three daughters and three sons. His mother, Margaret Jane, would remain at My Sweet Anna where her attentive granddaughters would dote over her as if she were Queen Victoria.

In July 1888, Matthew and Jane traveled to Los Angeles on the *Riverside, Santa Ana & Los Angeles* train and proceeded downtown to the Superior Court. Without ceremony, Matthew Gage, a native of Ireland, became a citizen of the United States. A small newspaper article referred to the fact that Matthew Gage had become a citizen, enabling him to become a director of any American corporation. Rules for citizenship included residency in the United States for five years, renouncing allegiance to a former country, and assumptions of obligations to your new country.

Willam Irving
Matthew Gage's Brother-in-law

After traveling five-and-a-half days from Kingston, Canada, Gage's relatives arrived in Riverside on August 13 in a deluxe, Pullman car. There were 24 people on board, including two unrelated families who disembarked in San Bernardino. The Robert Gage family, the Eliza Irving family and Robert Spooner, Matthew's nephew, were all warmly welcomed to Riverside. They brought trunks, wardrobes, household items and apparently planned to stay. Their special Pullman car remained parked on a spur track next to My Sweet Anna.[7]

Chatting relatives crossed the road to Matthew's home where they were amazed to discover a lovely garden spot with tall eucalyptus trees shading the driveway and the tall, gabled house. The visitors were excited at the sight of flourishing citrus trees and asked if the oranges were ready to eat. With the convenience of the nearby Pullman car, and the enlarged Gage house, family members settled into a comfortable summer routine until their rental houses became available.

William Irving's first view of Riverside included inspection of Section 30. He walked over the dusty mesa, checked the condition of the canal, and satisfied himself water could be conveyed beyond the Tequesquite Arroyo. Within days, he began surveying the barren land south of the big arroyo. William Irving was informed of Matthew's plan to develop a wide boulevard running the entire length of the tract and his survey plans included such a road. Matthew envisioned a streetcar line running along the median strip with the possibility of connecting to the Magnolia Avenue line. He recognized that such a sightseeing loop, from downtown and back, would be a significant tourist attraction allowing hundreds of visitors to take in Riverside's finest citrus groves and impressive mansions.

The name Victoria had been given to the vast tract of land formerly known as Carit's Tract in San Bernardino. William Irving and Matthew Gage wrote to Queen Victoria asking for her consent to name a grand avenue and access bridge, in her honor. In time, a letter from the Queen's private secretary arrived, indicating the Queen's permission to use her name. This highly treasured letter was proudly displayed in William Irving's home, Raeburn.[8]

Matthew, with the help of Robert and William, designed the divided road named Victoria Avenue. Lanes measured 18 to 20 feet wide and were divided by a 36 foot central median. Matthew named cross streets to honor family members; two for his wife, Jane and Gibson, (her maiden name) and six for his children, Anna, Frances, Horace, Maude, Marguerita and Robert. Other streets in Arlington Heights were named for his brother, John and John's wife Mary, and William and Irving for his sister Eliza's husband.

Matthew planned to border Victoria Avenue with pepper and eucalyptus trees that were fast growing and would act as windbreaks for citrus groves. His purpose was to enhance this section of town with a divided road that would surpass the beauty of Magnolia Avenue. Citizens of Riverside were convinced that their town was destined to become "more of a paradise under the Gage Canal and the development of Arlington Heights."[9]

Matthew had long realized the need for a convenient road from downtown Riverside to his Arlington Heights property. During the winter months, the big arroyo was filled with rushing water from surrounding canyons making a steep hillside road through the arroyo impractical. Both Priestley Hall, the owner of Hall's Addition on the south side of the Tequesquite Arroyo, and Matthew Gage wanted a bridge over the deep arroyo for better access to their properties. In December 1888, the two men proposed a triple lane bridge for the Hall's Addition Railroad, carriages, and walkers. Priestley Hall donated land in the Tequesquite Arroyo and property for a short road from the bridge to connect with Matthew's Arlington Heights land, starting at Victoria Avenue, near Myrtle Street.[10] This project was delayed, however, as Matthew Gage had other pressing problems. Determined entry men were continuing to dispute his claim to Section 30.

Real estate sales remained stable and merchants hoped that the 1888 winter tourist season would be as profitable as most previous years. Railroads continued to advertise free excursions to Riverside, stimulating interest with band music and free food. Out-of-town real estate agents, however, fearing the loss of sales sometimes resorted to false advertising and other unethical practices to divert tourists from Riverside.

Nevertheless, land in the Albert White Addition, Castleman Addition, and in Priestley Hall's Addition attracted potential buyers and business was good. The White and Castleman Additions sold home sites with piped water stored in a brick reservoir, filled with Gage Canal water. The Gage Canal furnished ample water to these new developments and Matthew continued drilling new wells in his artisan tract. During the fall of 1888, he had 36 artesian wells, mostly capped, and enough water to irrigate 12,000 acres. At the time, he was servicing 1,206 acres of citrus groves, vineyards, fields of alfalfa and summer crops, in addition to residential developments.[11]

The 1888 Citrus Fair, held in the Pavilion, was a tremendous success as thousands of out-of-town visitors wandered through the wooden structure brightly decorated in evergreens and flowers. Attractive arrangements of oranges, lemons, limes, raisins and dried fruit were displayed on tables covered with patriotic bunting. Matthew Gage had his own decorated booth. He displayed his home grown oranges and passed out brochures announcing the extension of the Gage Canal. He had decorative maps printed in San Francisco depicting sketches of Arlington Heights with artesian wells, orange groves, and the long flume over the big arroyo. Large signs announced, "It's the best orange land in the state and the grandest operation in southern California. Water to be delivered April 2, 1888."[12]

Two months after the fair, the six-year old Pavilion was totally destroyed by fire. Smoke and flames engulfed the wooden building from one end to the other, sending cinders as far as Box Springs Mountain, several miles away.[13] Everyone in town gave thanks for the absence of a strong wind as smoldering embers could have spread the fire to other downtown buildings and beyond. Firemen pumped water from the Riverside Water Company canal and after many hours controlled the fire.

With the Pavilion destroyed, the town lacked a civic meeting place and Charles M. Loring of Minnesota proposed a combination office building and opera house on the site of the former Pavilion. Loring, a wealthy man who spent his winters at the Glenwood Hotel, had an affinity for Riverside and its development, considering it to be his second home. He offered to provide rooms for city offices if officials agreed to rent space for ten years at a rate of $2,000 annually. Agreements were confirmed and construction began at the end of 1888. The prospect of having an opera house in Riverside delighted

Elegant Interior of the Loring Opera House.

John and Mary Gage, talented musicians, and Matthew and Jane, music connoisseurs. The Loring Opera House opened in January 1890, with Frank Miller as manager and booking agent.

Reverend J. B. Stewart, of Des Moines, Iowa, arrived in Riverside in 1888 in search of better climate. He was getting along in years but still had a reputation as one of the ablest orators in California. The Presbyterian minister attracted large congregations at Sunday sermons, Sunday school, Bible classes, and evening services.

Local newspapers reported the Iowan's growing popularity and supported efforts to erect a $20,000 church for the Reverend "who would fill it every Sunday." The Gage family embraced the idea of a church downtown as a more convenient location than the Magnolia Avenue church. In spite of his popularity, within a year the Reverend Stewart resigned "desiring rest and freedom from pastoral care."[14] The congregation was sorry to see him leave, but the proposal for a new church had been cast. The Presbyterians relied on visiting pastors until a permanent preacher received a call.

After several futile attempts, C. O. Perrine succeeded in organizing an association interested in creating a new cemetery. He sold his Pachappa Hill property to the new Olivewood Cemetery Company, becoming its principal stockholder. Originally, only 25 acres of 75 were subdivided into burial plots varying in price from $16 to $100 each. The selling point was its quiet, peaceful location where "neither a street nor railroad will ever run through it due to its topography."[15] Perrine landscaped the rocky slopes with a variety of trees and shrubs, greatly enhancing the property.

Burial plots were maintained by the cemetery association for a yearly fee, but owners had the option to care for their own. The Gage Canal furnished free water, under pressure, to the entire 75 acres. Matthew Gage was highly praised for his generosity and in return received a generous family plot located on a slight knoll above the main road. He had a huge stone marker installed with just the letters GAGE and Edith Anna's remains were transferred there. Twelve years later, Matthew enlarged the family plot, paying $700 for additional land.

During the fall of 1888, Riverside experienced a decline in real estate transactions, followed by rising interest rates. Those who had previously invested heavily in property soon realized that their transactions were nothing more than paper profits with little real capital involved. In contrast to the buying hysteria of the past several years, property owners began selling at any price, glutting the market with lots, orchards, and subdivision property. Matthew Gage disregarded the slumping market and continued to speculate on escalating prices, convinced that Arlington Heights property was superior to any other in southern California. While Matthew dealt with a fluctuating real estate market, his wife had her hands full tending to the children.

Jane called on Doctor Fannie Williams when Horace came down with a high fever. A lady doctor was quite a novelty in Riverside, even though her specialty was providing care for women and children.[16] Jane believed it appropriate to engage a female doctor for Margaret, now a young lady of 18, and Maude who was maturing rapidly. The boys and babies didn't seem to mind who made them feel better but Matthew relied on the good advice of his friend, Joseph Jarvis.

As a regular member of Riverside's Young Men's Christian Association, Matthew attended dedication ceremonies of the new building next to the Glenwood Hotel. The three-story structure had been constructed and furnished from donations and pledges. Unfortunately, many pledges had been cancelled due to the decline in land sales. Matthew, Jane, and the children became interested in a new concept of educational classes called child-garten or kindergarten offered by the YMCA. This new theory was described as "a garden where little children are the plants to be trained and nourished under the care of a good gardener." Kindergarten supposedly promoted harmonious development of mind and body.[17] Although the family realized advantages of early education, they did not participate. Matthew Gage seldom attended adult activities in the new building, but every week he drove his family to the Sunday services of the Calvary Presbyterian Church held in assembly halls of the YMCA.

Jane and Matthew discussed their children's education and concluded that public schools were not teaching the comprehensive subjects they desired. They decided not to enroll their children in the new high school under construction, considering its proximity to Chinatown's detrimental environment. Consequently Matthew, his brother Robert and brother-in-law William Irving, hired private teachers to educate their children. One month students met at Matthew Gage's house on Fourteenth Street, the following month at William Irving's house on Fourteenth and Main streets and

Riverside's 1887 YMCA Building on Main Street

then at Robert's house on the corner of Park and Date streets. The Irving - Gage cousins, who were together at school and at home, cultivated strong bonds and lasting unions.

During the transitional period of declining land sales, several important and distinguished investigative committees came to town searching for general public information. Matthew Gage, Riverside's new visionary and local hero, was a member of Riverside's Board of Trade, comprised of prominent businessmen intent on publicizing and promoting the city's prosperity and rich resources. When a distinguished

Englishman named David Lubin requested a conference with members of the organization, there was much speculation about his visit. The meeting was called to order in the parlors of the Glenwood Hotel and, after a short business meeting, the guest of honor was introduced.

Mr. Lubin emphasized the importance of world markets to the citrus industry such as London. He stated that the production of cultivated fruits in Italy and Spain could not compare to California's superior quality and high yield.[18] The State Board of Trade had voted to send an exhibition of the state's products to London in order to establish new foreign markets. Matthew made the motion to endorse the effort and Frank Miller seconded the motion.

Influential United State senators and department directors also visited Riverside. Prominent citizens acted as hosts and greeted their special trains, transporting guests to the Glenwood Hotel in their private buggies. These dignitaries were seeking information regarding Riverside's irrigated acreage and asked many questions. Matthew, the best informed in the gathering, answered their questions competently and diplomatically. He stated that the Riverside area had a total of 21,000 irrigable acres, of which 12,000 acres were under cultivation or provided with actual water facilities. Acres irrigated under old canals came to 6,200. The Gage system irrigated 1,500 acres but could adequately service 7,800 additional acres. He claimed his system could be easily increased with flumes, aqueducts, and cement pipes. Annual cost for citrus irrigation water averaged $3 an acre per year and $1.50 annually for vineyards.

Matthew Gage was interviewed and questioned concerning his canal system and he proudly reported, "The Gage Canal is the longest and largest artificial water course in San Bernardino County. It begins at a point four miles above the mouth of Warm Creek and nine miles below the canyon opening. The grade slope is about two feet per mile throughout with sliding wooden gates, 15 tunnels and 13 flumes. Many artesian wells are capped and ready for use when the Santa Ana River water becomes insufficient."[19]

The visitors, members of the Arid Land Commission touring the state to gather information about different methods of irrigation, were impressed by Matthew Gage's frank figures and knowledgeable report. They were driven along Magnolia Avenue to inspect a number of flourishing citrus groves where the dignitaries had visual proof of the magic of water.[20] Due to his magnificent canal, Matthew Gage acquired celebrity status.

CHAPTER 6

Matthew and his family realized that it would take a great deal more money to develop Arlington Heights. He had spent more than $200,000 building his canal, and his indebtedness was in excess of $800,000. Reasonable estimates to improve Arlington Heights required another half million dollars. Southern California banks were rapidly foreclosing on properties and reluctant to lend money, especially to one with huge liabilities.

Matthew was desperate. He wrote a detailed letter to Wilson Crewdson in London, recalling their encounter at the Glenwood Hotel during Crewdson's 1885 visit to Riverside. He cited their conversation concerning the construction of an irrigation canal and the Englishman's generous offer to participate in the project. Matthew outlined his intention to develop hundreds of acres with his expanded irrigation system and confessed his need for financing. Mr. Crewdson replied that he was fully invested in England, but thanked Mr. Gage for the correspondence and wished him well.

With a decline in tourist travel, railroads were offering reduced fares to California. They sought to lure potential buyers to their vast land holdings hoping to increase population and development along their right-of-way. Competition escalated, resulting in lower fares for all travelers. One such bargain fare extended beyond the U. S. border and caught the eye of Matthew Gage. A *California Southern Pacific Railroad* poster offered passage from California to Liverpool, England, for $65.[1]

Matthew, disappointed and dejected with Mr. Crewdson's response, decided to personally present his proposal to the Englishman. With Jane's encouragement, and a reasonable fare, he left Riverside in October 1889, crossing the Atlantic Ocean in six days on the steamer Etrurita.[2] Matthew's impetuous trip was evidence of his urgency for financial assistance, without which he would lose everything. He was thoroughly convinced that the development of Arlington Heights would generate substantial profits and he wanted to assure Mr. Credwson that his project was a legitimate business proposal.

Matthew met with Mr. Crewdson in his well appointed office and after a friendly discussion concerning Riverside's prosperity, he described his new enterprise and plans to complete the project. He enthusiastically expressed his belief that Riverside's citrus industry would continue to expand, with national and international markets, increasing production and, ultimately, land sales. After detailing his visionary plans, Mr. Crewdson introduced Matthew to his uncle, Theodore Waterhouse, senior partner of the international accounting firm of Price, Waterhouse Company. This London firm, organized by Edwin Waterhouse and Samuel Price in 1849, was considered to be one of the most prestigious in England.[3]

On December 13, 1889, Gage and the two Englishmen considered the Arlington Heights development, estimating costs and calculating profits from future land sales. During their discussions, the Englishmen outlined a preliminary proposal to purchase Gage's assets after organizing a group of investors. Although nothing was concluded, or put in writing, Matthew was encouraged by their serious attitude and interest.

Following their congenial conference, Matthew returned to Riverside to spend the Christmas holidays with his family. Christmas was a happy time in the Gage house, with brighter prospects for the New Year, 1890.

Soon after Matthew left London, Mr. Waterhouse sent a telegram to George Sneath, a Price, Waterhouse Company representative working in California. He was instructed to discreetly inspect Matthew Gage's Riverside property located south of the big arroyo and to confirm Matthew's character and standing in the community. Sneath followed orders and, after several days of investigating the canal, Section 30 and land yet to be developed, his conclusions were favorable. His

Gage Children - Frances, age 3; Robert, age 7; Horace, age 10; Anna, age 4

report found the Arlington Heights subdivision to be a major project with great potential and profitability.[4] Furthermore, Matthew Gage was a pillar of the community, a church member in good standing, opposed to liquor and saloons. The assessment roll of the City of Riverside for 1889 listed Matthew Gage's assessed valuation at $60,955.[5] His only blemish was the ongoing lawsuit concerning his claim to Section 30 and until he obtained clear title, it could not be sold.

Mr. Sneath gave a short account recognizing Riverside's favorable prosperity. He believed the navel orange industry would surely increase land values. Civic minded citizens were erecting impressive buildings including a three-story Young Men's Christian Association structure, a large brick high school, a new landscaped cemetery, and an ornate opera house named for Charles Loring. These public improvements would inspire genteel citizens to purchase property and to settle in the progressive, refined community of Riverside. Apparently Mr. Sneath's detailed report pleased Wilson Crewdson and his potential investors.

During the early hours of February 11, 1890, 60-year-old Christopher Columbus Miller died suddenly. He had appeared spry and energetic as recently as the previous day. Private services, held on the day he died, took place in his Glenwood Hotel home at 3 o'clock in the afternoon. Friends were requested to meet an hour later in order to follow the hearse to Evergreen Cemetery for burial. The long, solemn parade included Matthew Gage, who had recently returned from London.[6] The Miller and Gage families had been close friends since 1881 and Matthew admired the late Mr. Miller, who had successfully surveyed and engineered his canal. Following C. C. Miller's funeral, rumors circulated that Matthew was involved in an important transaction, details of which were not disclosed.

In March 1890, Matthew returned to the London offices of Wilson Crewdson. There, he signed legal documents conveying his Arlington Heights property and his irrigation canal, including all water rights, to an English investment group incorporated as the Riverside Trust Company, Limited. The new company, headed by Crewdson and Waterhouse, was capitalized at $1,250,000 American dollars. The purchase agreement included the Gage Canal water system, Matthew's 7171 acres of land known as the Victoria Tract, and 4790 acres known as Arlington Heights. In return, Matthew was to receive stock in the new Trust company, acquiring 800 A-shares valued at $50 each and 900 B-shares valued at one dollar each. In addition, the contract stated that he would receive two-thirds of profits after payment of six percent dividends to stockholders. Furthermore, the nine-member board of directors hired Matthew to manage Arlington Heights at an annual salary of $10,000 and per contract he became a director on the board.[7] With the introduction of English capital, Matthew assumed huge profits would be forthcoming from land sales and the development of Arlington Heights.

In his eagerness to reduce his indebtedness and to profit from the orderly development of Arlington Heights, Matthew signed numerous lengthy documents. Unfortunately, he had little legal advice and no knowledge of English law, which was more complex than American statutes. Four years later, he testified that the 1889 preliminary offer and the legal binding contract of 1890 were inconsistent and he had been deceived.

On March 30, 1890, representatives of the Riverside Trust Company, Limited filed deeds of land and water ownership in the San Bernardino County Recorders Office. The English company took possession of Gage's canal and water rights and his Riverside properties, including everything except his ten-acre home place, My Sweet Anna and Section 30, pending a clear title.

Elmer Holmes, editor of the *Riverside Daily Press*, wrote:

We understand the wealthy syndicate that recently became interested in the fine tract of land under the Gage system will shortly commence work in earnest in improving their magnificent property. One of the first things the company plans to do is build a fine bridge across Tequesquite Arroyo and grade another wide and beautiful street, to be called Victoria Avenue, down the valley, parallel with Magnolia, along which a car line will be run. The commencement of this great work, together with the amount of residence building and tree planting now planned indicate without doubt that a period of renewed growth for Riverside is approaching.[8]

Matthew Gage's million dollar sale made news throughout southern California. His family, grateful to have his debts reduced, were happy to have him home. Community leaders were amazed, and enthralled, having a foreign company helping to beautify their town. Despite the decrease in land sales throughout the state, Matthew was confident that the beauty of Arlington Heights, the increasing importance of citrus production, and prospects of an elite settlement would stimulate extraordinary land sales.

On June 12, 1890, Matthew received the following correspondence:

> Dear Sir:
> Your friends, and neighbors, who have watched your struggles and final success in the completion of the splendid canal system that bears your name, and records your enterprise and courage, desire to give public expression of their appreciation of your labors for the material development of this valley by tendering you a banquet at such time as you may be pleased to name.
> Respectfully yours,
> Joseph Jarvis, A. J. Twogood, Priestley Hall, O. T. Dyer, (and thirteen other prominent businessmen.)

Matthew Gage's response came four days later.

> Gentlemen:
> I beg leave to acknowledge the receipt of your communication of the 12th instant, tendering on behalf of the people of Riverside, a banquet to me at such time as would suit my convenience; and in reply would name Wednesday, the 25th of June, 1890. Thanking you very cordially for this public expression of your kind regard and appreciation of my humble efforts in

developing the resources of this beautiful valley. I am, very respectfully,
Your obedient servant,
Matthew Gage[9]

On the eventful evening of June 25, 1890, 46-year old Matthew Gage was ceremoniously acknowledged for his heroic accomplishments in energetically and physically facilitating the beautification of the City of Riverside. Distinguished guests attending the grand Gage Banquet arrived in their finest carriages, driving into the brightly decorated courtyard of the Glenwood Hotel. As they entered the reception lobby, decorated with brightly colored Chinese lanterns, patrons were greeted with musical renditions played by a 17-piece orchestra.

Matthew and Jane (who was again pregnant) accompanied her sister, Aggie Gibson, his sister Sarah Spooner, and his 79-year-old mother, Margaret Gage, all from Kingston, Canada. This was an auspicious occasion for the entire family, a night long remembered.

At 9:30, white gloved ushers escorted guests to their assigned tables in the dining room decorated in draped flags, colorful flowers, sprays of evergreens, and placards. At the head of the room appeared the motto: RIVERSIDE TRUST COMPANY - AMERICAN ENERGY AND ENGLISH CAPITAL. Draped beneath the sign were crossed Union Jack and American flags. The name GAGE, in radiant green branches, had a background frame of bright white flowers. Magnificent floral arrangements were placed on well-appointed tables accommodating 161 guests.

Placed on each fine, china plate was a bound souvenir program announcing "Testimonial Banquet to Matthew Gage by citizens of Riverside, California, Wednesday June 25, 1890." The handsome booklet contained a good likeness of Matthew, the extensive bill of fare, and a list of Toast Masters. The late evening meal included chicken, shrimp, turkey, ham, tongue, lobster, and a choice of six desserts.

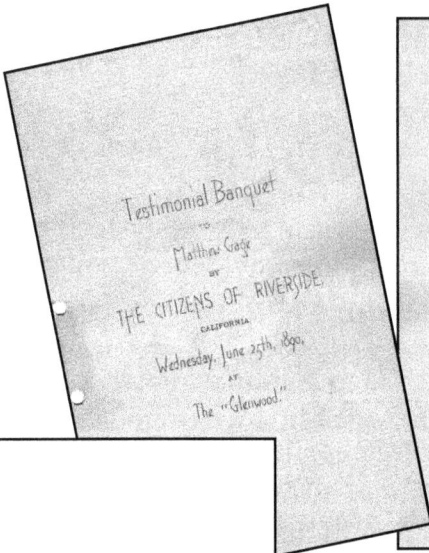

Testimonial Banquet

TO

Matthew Gage

BY

THE CITIZENS OF RIVERSIDE

CALIFORNIA

Wednesday, June 25th, 1890.

AT

The "Glenwood."

Menu.

Blue Points

Potage a la Reine

Olives

Broiled Spring Chicken
Serpentine Potatoes

Shrimp Patties a la Creme

Cold Turkey with Aspec Jelly
Cold Boiled Ham
Smoked Beef Tongue

Fresh Lobsters en Mayonaise
Chicken Salad

Strawberry Sherbet

Vanilla Ice Cream   Fruited Jellies
Assorted Cake   Fruits

Snowflake Crackers   Cheese

Black Coffee

Toasts.

OUR GUEST—(MATTHEW GAGE)
Response by W. J. McIntyre.

RIVERSIDE—
Response by H. B. Everest.

RIVERSIDE TRUST CO. (LIMITED)
Response by Matthew Gage.

RIVERSIDE WATER CO.—
Response by Dr. J. Jarvis.

THE ORANGE AND RAISIN INDUSTRY—
Response by F. R. Skelley.

THE GAGE CANAL SYSTEM—
Response by A. H. Naftzger.

THE LADIES—
Response by O. T. Dyer.

THE PRESS—
Response by E. W. Holmes.

EDUCATION—
Response by Rev. R. H. Hartley.

A. H. NAFTZGER. *Toast Master.*

Testimonial Banquet Program at Glenwood on June 25, 1890

At the conclusion of the lavish banquet, Toast Master A. H. Naftzer took charge and stated the large representative gathering emphatically confirmed the people of Riverside appreciated "our fellow citizen, Matthew Gage." After nine complimentary toasts and glowing speeches, the guest of honor took the floor. He pleasantly reviewed events concerning his arrival in Riverside, nine years earlier, and described his first sight of the small town. A fond memory was the welcome greetings of his transplanted Canadian friends. After other reminisces, he bestowed loving praise upon his wife Jane, "who always aided and encouraged me in my pursuits. I admit no small share of my success is due to her helpful confidence and support."[10]

It became too late in the evening to read the many complimentary letters and telegrams delivered to the Glenwood. After numerous good wishes and accolades, the Gage family retired to My Sweet Anna in high spirits and with many memories. His hard work, timely vision, and constant persistence had been acknowledged by his peers. In retrospect, he felt blessed and humbled. Matthew's future years would not always be so joyful and rewarding.

In September, a new member came to live in the Gage house when Katherine MacKenzie was born. Matthew and Jane then had seven living children.

One of the early projects advocated by the English syndicate involved construction of a bridge spanning the Tequesquite Arroyo, providing access from town to their land. Another beneficial improvement had to do with grading a double lane road to be called Victoria Avenue. It was planned to have a streetcar line installed in the center divider of Victoria Avenue, similar to that on Magnolia Avenue. While the Englishmen were considering these projects, Matthew kept busy supervising street grading, William Irving continued to survey acreage into smaller parcels, and Robert Gage worked on extending the Gage Canal. Matthew proceeded to secure rights-of-way across the Tequesquite Arroyo and land connecting to the Trust Company property. Priestley Hall owned land in the arroyo and readily donated a right-of-way for a bridge that would provide access to his subdivision along the south side of the arroyo.[11]

In response to an economic depression that engulfed the nation in the 1890s, the Riverside Trust Company did little advertising, resulting in few land sales. English investors anticipated that producing citrus groves and landscaped home sites would be more

Katherine MacKenzie Gage, Age 4

desirable and saleable in the future. Funds derived from meager sales were used for improvements, with only small, or no, dividends returned to stockholders.

Under Matthew's supervision, the Trust Company continued sinking wells in the Victoria Tract to insure a sufficient supply of water for Arlington Heights. In 1887, 14 wells produced 600 miner's inches and, by 1892, there were 55 wells producing 1793 miner's inches. In 1891, there were 46 flowing wells and many more capped for future use.

Following the lead of the Riverside Trust Company, another group of English capitalists purchased the San Jacinto Tin Mining Company south of Riverside. The San Jacinto Estate Limited of London, England, acquired 50,000 acres that had been in litigation for over 20 years. The tin ore was reputed to be better than any from mines in Cornwall and, consequently, metal merchants in Cornwall and Liverpool purchased most of the 500,000 shares of common stock at $5 each. Englishmen were investing heavily in southern California, especially near Riverside.[12]

Regardless of the depression that limited Riverside's growth, the young community continued to blossom. City officials imported date palm trees from northern Africa and planted them along public streets. School enrollment reached a total of 700 students, including 108 enrolled in the new high school. Raisins remained a profitable crop, even though citrus groves were rapidly replacing vineyards. Residents developed a bathing resort at Spring Brook near the Santa Ana River and a tennis club officially organized as the Casa Blanca Tennis Club with facilities on Monroe Street. The progressive town, with a population of less than 5,000, was gaining a national reputation as the center of the southern California Orange Belt.

Articles of incorporation for the Gage Canal Company were filed with the county clerk on August 28, 1890. Directors were listed as Matthew Gage, William Irving, Robert Gage, Austin Henry Jennings, all of Riverside, and W. Crewdson of London, England. Fifty thousand shares of stock at $50 each, was issued to be used for distribution and allotment of water without profit to the company. The Gage Canal Company was authorized to buy, own, hire, and make covenants and agreements with the Riverside Trust Company, Limited.[13] With the filing of corporate papers, Matthew Gage no longer owned the extensive irrigation system that he had created.

The Gage family had been deeply involved in their church activities and when the Calvary Presbyterians decided to build their new building, Matthew eagerly participated. On September 29, 1890, architect Adam C. Willard signed a contract to design a church to be erected on the corner of Lime and Ninth streets. Carpentry work was awarded to J .E. Porter, brick and mason work to H. A. Knapp, and plumbing to Mr. Ormand. Knapp used a new leveling tool enabling the foundation to be absolutely accurate. Due to delays in receiving materials, it took nearly a year to complete the building and the congregation continued to meet in the YMCA.

The completed church reflected a Norman style of architecture with a high square corner tower. Heavy plate glass doors opened into an enormous auditorium capable of seating 450 people. An arched ceiling with decorative beams added to the beauty and vast feeling of the sanctuary. A jeweled, cut-glass window depicted the seal of a Scottish Presbyterian church with the inscription, "Always burning but never consumed." It was deemed the most elegant church in the city with pews of solid oak, Brussels carpets, perfect ventilation, and a convenient floor plan.[14] Formal dedication ceremonies took place the end of November, 1891.

Matthew remained active during the 1890s, consumed in managing countless improvements to the vast barren Arlington Heights tract. Dressed in sturdy work trousers, high laced boots, and a wide-brimmed hat, he supervised crews grading streets and leveling fields. Thousands of rabbits were made homeless and frequently ended up in stew pots. The extended canal had to be cemented, and steel pipes installed to reach each parcel. Matthew ordered 500,000 young navel orange trees from Florida to be planted in the fertile soil.

Brothers William and Edward Gullick purchased 40 acres in Arlington Heights in 1891 and established a successful nursery business near Washington Street. They built a modest farmhouse and landscaped their property with imposing pepper, eucalyptus, and palm trees. The Riverside Trust Company ordered 150,000 citrus trees from the Gullick Nursery. The shipment came from Florida and was thoroughly treated to eliminate insect pests.

Ethan Allen Chase, and three of his sons, had operated a nationally known nursery business in Rochester, New York before moving to Riverside in the 1890s. They purchased citrus property throughout southern California and became the largest growers in Riverside, establishing their own packinghouse known as the National Orange Company.

Calvary Presbyterian Church, Lime and Ninth Streets, 1891

Chase enterprises developed and sold land as well as nursery stock.[15]

Matthew purchased property in Arlington Heights in 1891, Block 65, for $40,000. The Victoria Avenue property near Jane Street was ideally located on a slight knoll affording a spectacular view. He planted 20 acres in young navel orange trees with plans to develop the remaining acreage at a later date. Matthew intended to pay the Riverside Trust Company $40,000 from his stock dividends.[16]

It was a great day in April 1891 when President Benjamin Harrison and his wife, Caroline, visited Riverside. Even though his journey through town was short, he received a festive reception as the nation's chief executive. His presidential train arrived near the English syndicate's tin mines at four o'clock where distinguished dignitaries welcomed the guests. The president's special carriage was covered with flowers and conveyed the party down Magnolia Avenue. At a designated location, the carriage turned into a well-groomed orange grove where the president picked ripe oranges from the trees without rising from his seat. Hundreds of cheering

Main Street Decorated for President Harrison's Visit to Riverside

people lined the Avenue anxious to see the president and both children and adults waved small American flags as he passed by. The caravan drove beneath a huge arch bearing the word WELCOME spelled in brightly colored flowers. When the parade approached the new high school on Fourteenth Street, hundreds of school children shouted friendly greetings and tossed flower petals.

Matthew and his family stood in front of the Glenwood Hotel with the Miller family as President Harrison's carriage came to a stop. Nine-year-old Allis Miller presented Mrs. Harrison with a basket of radiant flowers. Ladies of the Women's Christian Temperance Union delivered two baskets of oranges to President Harrison as his entourage headed for the depot to his waiting train.[17] Sometime later, the President remarked that Riverside had the best oranges he had ever eaten.

Rights-of-way to Victoria Avenue had been granted on January 29, 1891, but work progressed slowly due to long delays. Directors of the Trust Company had decided to postpone construction of the road until a vital bridge could be erected across the big arroyo. The Trust Company announced in February that work on the bridge would begin soon; however, nothing happened. Riverside's rainy season arrived and then the hot summer season before any action took place.

Construction finally started in September when lumber and cement were stacked in the arroyo. Within two months, an impressive bridge crossed the Tequesquite Arroyo, a vital link joining downtown Riverside with Arlington Heights. William Irving, chief engineer for the Riverside Trust Company, designed the cantilevered truss bridge with a 30 foot wide plank floor. Irving's perceptive engineering skills provided granite block foundations on bedrock to support the 560-foot-long, 60-foot-high structure that could support a weight of 300 pounds per square foot.[18] During construction, local residents visited the site, observing agile workmen climb and work around the wooden braces supporting the bridge.

It was a beautiful Thanksgiving Day in 1891 when the magnificent $12,000 structure across the Tequesquite Arroyo, known as the Victoria Bridge, was officially dedicated. Wooden railings were draped in bright streamers and layers of bunting and flag poles at either end displayed American flags. When the November afternoon sun filtered through the skeleton trestle frame, it outlined the bridge against the arroyo floor.

Ceremonial activities began at the north end, where a wide red carpet covered the dusty entry to the bridge. Hundreds of carriages, buggies and bicycles were parked near both ends of the bridge, where throngs of pedestrians waited to cross. William Irving acted as master of ceremonies, for he had drawn plans for the bridge and supervised its construction.[19]

He invited Mr. Phoemix, on behalf of the mechanics who constructed the bridge, to drive the first of three remaining spikes into the last wooden plank. Irving called upon a list of impressive citizens to tap the second spike into place. The third shiny, gilded spike had been reserved for Margaret Orr Gage, Matthew's 81-year old mother. When she carefully tapped the metal spike, applause and band music filled the air. The sudden uproar frightened the waiting horses before men and boys rushed to calm them down.

William Irving turned the ceremony over to his brother-in-law, Matthew Gage, manager of the Trust Company, who had long envisioned such a bridge. The jovial Irishman told the crowd:

> "Building this bridge might seem to be selfish in that I might enhance the value of every lot in Arlington Heights. My motto is Riverside, first, last, and always. I want but one commercial center, Riverside. I have much pleasure in declaring this bridge open to traffic, use it, and enjoy it."

Another boisterous outburst frightened the horses again. After completion of the formalities, uniformed band members stood ready to head the possession south across the new Victoria Bridge. As the band marched along the plank bridge, 185 carriages and wagons and countless walkers followed. The first to cross was the decorated buggy conveying Margaret Gage. Her numerous Irving and Gage grandchildren pulled the carriage across the bridge, followed by hundreds of enthusiastic participants.[20] The parade proceeded along a narrow, dirt road leading to the beginning of Victoria Avenue.

Local citizens were surprised at the number of newly planted citrus groves and the many new streets and roads. The parade stopped at Camp Arlington, the Trust Company's temporary headquarters near Adams and Victoria Avenue. Several small, frame buildings used for offices and tool storage were open to the public and Trust Company officials provided lemonade and cookies. The new bridge was proclaimed a credit to the city and became a special source of pride for all Riverside citizens. Thanksgiving Day had been spectacular for Matthew and his family.

Later, in January 1895, the Riverside Trust Company presented the Victoria Bridge to the City of Riverside, though

Hall's Addition Street Railway.

the official deed was not recorded until 1898. Perhaps the city was better prepared to cope with ongoing bridge repairs and the installation of a new streetcar system.

On Sunday, November 29, 1891, three days after the official opening of the Victoria Bridge, the Gage family attended the formal dedication of Riverside's Calvary Presbyterian Church. Hundreds of people, of all denominations, gathered in the new structure to hear Dr. McKenzie, a noted theologian. The congregation also attended services to hear the $5,000 Roosevelt pipe organ Matthew Gage had donated to the church. A few years later, Jane Gage rededicated the organ in memory of her departed children.[21]

CHAPTER 7

During the Christmas holidays, Mother Gage became increasingly frail and often excused herself from attending family gatherings. As the new year began, her declining health became obvious to Matthew and others, prompting a consultation with her physician, Joseph Jarvis. Following a subsequent examination of the 81-year-old dowager, Dr. Jarvis concluded that she suffered from multiple infirmities of old age and that there was little that could be done, other than to keep her comfortable.

Margaret Jane Orr Gage died peacefully on January 24, 1892. Services were held two days later in the Calvary Presbyterian Church. Often referred to as the "Gage" church, in reference to Matthew's founding membership, Mother Gage had last attended the new facility a month earlier, on the occasion of its formal dedication.

Mother Gage's simple casket was escorted down the center aisle by her three sons, Matthew, Robert, and John, and by her son-in-law William Irving. Soft organ music could be heard as pallbearers slowly approached the altar surrounded in beautiful baskets of colorful flowers and greenery.

Reverends Henry B. Gage and R. H. Hartley led the large assembly in prayer followed by spiritual recitations and remembrances of family and friends. Each one emphasized the esteemed legacy that Margaret Gage had bestowed to her family, "a rich gift of responsibility, strength of character, and a gentle spirit."[1] A solemn 48-year-old Matthew sat beside his wife, Jane, and their seven children: Margaret, 22; Maude, 16; Horace, 12; Robert, 9; Anna, 6; Frances, 5; and Katherine, 3.

A long carriage procession followed the horse-drawn hearse to Olivewood Cemetery where grieving relatives and friends gathered. As the casket was slowly lowered, family members scattered dried rose petals into the open grave. She had indeed left a lineage of gifted personalities and diligent individuals, including her ambitious son Matthew.

The historic real estate boom of the 1880s had run its course by the early 1890s, as sales began to diminish. The ensuing years witnessed a worldwide economic depression. Banking institutions ceased easy credit and applied high interest rates.[2] The nine directors of the Riverside Trust Company, Limited were highly regarded and experienced in international banking and investments. With the prospects of an approaching European recession, the English directors ceased sales of Arlington Heights property in favor of developing the land themselves. They expected revenue from citrus crops to be a profitable and safe investment in southern California. The decisions of the directors and Matthew Gage's motivations differed greatly, as he was in need of immediate funds.

Nevertheless, Matthew continued in his efforts to improve the Heights with the assistance of his brother, Robert, and, of his brother-in-law, William Irving. Matthew's relatives were employees of the Riverside Trust Company, highly qualified professionals who had no financial ties with the company. They assisted in expanding and developing Arlington Heights and supervised cementing the Gage Canal, planting trees, grading new roads, and leveling land.

Franz Hosp, one of southern California's early landscape gardeners, was hired to manage the beautification of the development.[3] Hundreds of Washingtonia robusta palms and fast-growing eucalyptus trees were planted along both sides of Victoria Avenue and within the median strip. These contrasting trees provided both shade and ornamentation.

The Victoria School District was created in February 1892 to accommodate the few families in the area. The Riverside Trust Company donated a two-and-a-half acre site on Victoria Avenue near St. Lawrence Street. The land, valued at $10,000, was to be used for school purposes and would revert back to the Trust Company, if or when, it was no longer used for a school. The two-story frame building cost $6,500 to build and

Victoria School, Victoria Avenue near St. Lawrence Street, 1892

featured a central tower with a large school bell that could be heard throughout the neighborhood.[4] It was considered the finest school in town when it opened in October with 35 students.

Matthew, as manager of the Trust Company, agreed to allow a group of polo enthusiasts to use vacant land near the corner of Victoria Avenue and Van Buren Boulevard for a polo field. Polo, tennis, and golf had become popular as an increasing number of English families spent their winters in Riverside. To repay Matthew Gage for the use of the property, he was selected president of the Riverside Golf and Polo Club. Although he did not participate in either sport, his eldest daughters, Margaret and Maude, were athletically inclined and were members of the Casa Blanca Lawn Tennis Club.[5]

Casa Blanca Tennis Club Members ca. 1890s

After Henry Lockwood moved to New York, members of the Casa Blanca Tennis Club purchased several acres on Adams Street, east of Magnolia Avenue, and, in 1891, built six dirt courts and a one-story, frame clubhouse with a wide front porch. The tennis club became one of Riverside's most important social organizations where the younger generation participated in athletic activities and mature generations socialized. Afternoon tea, an English custom, became the setting for discriminating romantic encounters under the watchful eyes of dignified matrons.[6]

Twenty-year-old Margaret and 15-year-old Maude joined the elite club where they became adept tennis players and befriended members their own ages. They attended tournaments, dances, and costume parties in the modest clubhouse and established many enduring friendships, both male and female. From their home on Fourteenth Street, they rode on Priestley Hall's horse-drawn streetcar, known as Hall's Addition Railroad, that connected to the *Riverside and Arlington*

Railroad on Main Street. This horse-drawn car traveled over Brockton Avenue, along the median strip of Magnolia Avenue and to Adams Street, where the girls disembarked. Matthew and Jane were pleased to have their daughters active in their church and participating in Riverside's social life.

Correspondence between Matthew and the Trust Company directors in London was carried out via telegraph, even though Riverside had inaugurated mail delivery in January. The Gage family received two daily mail deliveries conveyed by a mailman on horseback. Nevertheless, short, direct messages from each country were transmitted via Western Union offices. The English company continued to invest in improvements, expending little time or effort in marketing Arlington Heights. In the spring of 1892, Matthew left for London to attend a Board of Directors' meeting and to once again express his concerns over the lack of sales. He questioned vast expenditures for property development resulting in small dividends to B stock owners.

Riverside experienced several cases of diphtheria in March 1892 and Doctor W. B. Sawyer, the local health officer, issued warnings of the spread of the highly contagious disease. Many were unaware of this disease that had come to light ten years earlier. Doctor Sawyer noted that diphtheria could start with a sore throat and fever and cause swollen neck glands. Bacteria in the throat, nose and larynx could also affect the heart, causing a rapid pulse resulting in paralysis and sudden death. He stated that the greatest problem with diphtheria was the state of panic and fear it caused within the home. He recommended keeping patients quiet and to place a dish of bromine, a toxic salt water liquid in the sick room.[7]

Health department officials reported two cases of diphtheria in March and 26 in April. Public schools closed indefinitely and Sunday school classes were cancelled. Individuals were reluctant to gather in groups or to socialize, in accordance with Dr. Sawyer's prescribed precautions.

In spite of preventative measures undertaken in the Gage household, Robert Condit Gage died of diphtheria on

May 1, 1892, at the age of 9 years and 1 month. The family was in a state of shock with Matthew in London and six siblings residing in the house of sickness. The community extended deepest sympathy to Jane. The Robert Gage, John Gage and Irving families offered help, but were not permitted near the quarantined house. A black wreath, the symbol of death, hung on the front door. Young Robert was buried the following day in Olivewood Cemetery near his Grandmother Gage. Matthew would not know of his loss for some time.

One week later, on Saturday, May 7, Doctor Sawyer reported eight diphtheria cases in the city, including another patient in the Matthew Gage house. In the early morning of May 13, Horace James Gage died of diphtheria, aged 12 years, 2 months and 2 days. He had been a victim of the disease since his brother's death and every known remedy had been administered. The children of Robert Gage, John Gage and William Irving had gathered sweet smelling eucalyptus branches to be placed over door frames in the sick room as a disinfectant. John, the Chinese helper, had offered a leather pouch of dried leaves and unknown bones to clear the air of germs.

Horace had actually seemed to be feeling better on May 12, but took a turn for the worse and passed away at 2 a.m. The black wreath of death was once again displayed on the Gage's front door. Horace's private interment occurred later that same day at Olivewood Cemetery. Immediate burial was a local requirement for communicable diseases. Community leaders, good friends and the Gage-Irving families, extended sympathetic condolences of love and prayers to the family. The loss of her sons was devastating to Jane, and friends and family were concerned about her health and weak heart. Friendly church members reminded her she still had five daughters who needed her wise counsel and loving care.

Matthew returned to Riverside as soon as possible when he received a telegram with the sad news. He had lost his only sons and the future generations that might bear his name. His concern for Jane's health and surviving daughters kept him close to home during a two month period of mourning.

In July, Matthew met again with Mr. Crewdson and other directors of the Trust Company in England. When he left London, he realized there would be little or no change in the Trust Company's policy of continued planting and developing of citrus property. As Matthew crossed the Atlantic Ocean on his way home, the Associated Press released a late dispatch on August 2, 1892, to Riverside newspapers under the heading, A SECTION GONE:

> Matthew Gage's Desert Claim Lost. Under the U.S. Secretary of the Interior, the Land Commissioner reversed, rejected, canceled Gage's claim. He determined the Desert Land claim had not been complied with and reclamation of the land had not been accomplished within the time limit. Contestants were William E. Atwater, Otto Newman, and John J. Gunther.[8]

The day after the decision was handed down, William Atwater filled an affidavit and paid the fee to J. G. Bethune, Register of United States Land Office in Los Angeles, for his Homestead and Timber Culture entry to 112 acres of Section 30. This amounted to a quarter section near Eighth Street and Chicago Avenue, less part of an unusable arroyo near Canyon Crest Drive. Atwater lived on Chicago Avenue, near Eighth Street, with his wife and daughter and managed the Evergreen Nursery in East Riverside. He immediately purchased $100 worth of lumber, filling two wagon loads, and had it delivered to Section 30 in order to build a house on his new property. Within the week, John Gunther filed a Homestead claim to another quarter section of Section 30, located across the street from his house on Chicago Avenue.[9]

When Matthew arrived home, he learned that the Angel of Death had visited his household again on August 18, when Frances Gibson, age 4 years and 10 months, died.

An attack of diphtheria, contracted six weeks earlier, was the cause of death. She was laid to rest near her siblings and grandmother in Olivewood Cemetery.

With the death of three children within three-and-a-half months, Matthew became concerned about Jane's health and frame of mind. He consulted his friend Dr. Joseph Jarvis and asked him to take charge of her health and called upon Dr. Hartley, pastor of the Calvary Presbyterian Church, to provide her religious needs. The good pastor offered solace to the bereaved family, paying daily visits and consoling prayers. Later, Jane rededicated the melodious pipe-organ in the Calvary Church in memory of their children and in gratitude for the many prayers and condolences during their time of bereavement.

During the fall of 1892, Matthew kept busy supervising the cementing of his canal to improve water distribution and conservation. Crews worked east of Section 30 and in Arlington Heights during the winter months when the canal was not in use. Arlington Heights then embodied 1150 acres of planted citrus trees.

Gray Brothers of Los Angeles received the cementing contract for the Gage Canal and their 45-man crew completed 850 feet a day. They installed concrete bulkheads in strategic locations where metal gates lifted to allow water into side ditches. Matthew, as manager, watched over the men as they made grade changes and smoothed out slopes and canal floors for the approaching cement workers.

Earlier planted citrus groves began to produce marketable crops and the Riverside Trust Company hired Charles E. Maud, a likeable Englishman sportsman, to supervise and manage a new enterprise, the Riverside Orange Packing Company, shippers and packers of Arlington fruit. His brother, Horace, became foreman of the Orange Company.[10] The company's upper ranch consisted of 200 acres of citrus trees while the lower ranch near Victoria and Adams, covered 300 acres. Ranch headquarters were first located near Madison and Victoria avenues, closer to the Casa Blanca quarry and the *Santa Fe Railroad* station. A nursery, boarding house, stable, and office complex comprised the Arlington Camp. Resident workers were trained as irrigators, fumigators, or nurserymen. Laborers kept the canal clear of grass, moss, and debris.

The Trust Company also hired William Grant Fraser, a reliable young accountant, to keep the firm's Riverside books and financial statements in good

Franz Hosp

order. He reported directly to the London Board of Directors. Twenty-six-year-old John M. Mylne of Ottawa, Canada was hired as William Irving's assistant engineer and lived in the second Trust Company camp on the corner of Victoria Avenue and McAllister Street. The simple buildings contained small offices and separate living quarters for executives and laborers. Matthew Gage, Charles Maud, and William Fraser were headquartered here but worked independently of each other.

Another employee named John H. Newmarch arrived in Riverside from London bearing the title of Trust Company secretary. He opened a downtown office in the Rowell Building at Ninth and Main streets and no one could determine what his responsibilities entailed. It was concluded that he was a representative for Mr. Crewdson and directors of the Trust Company. The following year, when Mr. Newmarch returned to England, William G. Fraser became secretary-treasurer of the company.

Franz Hosp, the landscape gardener, utilized land surrounding the McAllister complex where he nurtured blue gum eucalyptus trees. These native Australian trees seeded themselves, were considered inexpensive, and were fast growing. Besides acting as excellent wind breaks for citrus groves, the ornamental trees required little attention and were also useful sources of fire wood and wood chips.

Matthew continued as manager but no longer supervised the entire operation for the Trust Company. Part of Matthew's work load was shifted to Charles Maud and Will Fraser, who handled separate interests of the Trust Company. There were certain times and instances when Matthew believed the new employees were appraising his judgment and evaluating his actions on behalf of the Board of Directors in London.

On the momentous day of March 31, 1893, Matthew Gage sent his letter of resignation as manager of the Riverside Trust Company, Limited, effective May 1, to London, England. This move was unexpected, but he reassured friends and associates that his retirement as manager was not his retirement from business. Local newspapers stated, ''Mr. Gage's retirement is said to be due to a difference of opinion in regard to what should be the policy of the company.''[11] Matthew recommended William Irving, his brother-in-law, to be the new manager of Arlington Heights.

Sixty-one year old Irving was familiar with every facet of the Arlington Heights development and had no financial interest in the Riverside Trust Company. He was well-educated as an architect and civil engineer and possessed a clear, analytical mind. He lived on Fourteenth Street with his wife, Eliza, and their six children, Elizabeth Brow, Margaret Eva, Kathleen, William Gage, Robert and Norman.

As a previous consultant and engineer for the Gage Canal and Arlington Heights, his expertise was invaluable and William Irving replaced Matthew as manager, a position he ably fulfilled for seven years. Irving realized Matthew's frustrations with the company and his efforts to obtain better returns from his stock. After his retirement, Matthew focused on obtaining additional A-shares to gain higher yields.

Matthew's last day as manager of the Riverside Trust Company, Limited, coincided with the opening of the World's Columbian Exposition in Chicago, a celebration to commemorate the 400th anniversary of the discovery of America. New York, Washington, and St. Louis had vied to host the international affair, but Congress had voted in favor of Chicago. Commonly referred to as the Chicago World's Fair, the event had been scheduled to open on October 21, 1892, the traditional anniversary of Columbus stepping ashore on a West Indian Island. It officially opened, however, on May 1, 1893.

Each state had its own building and California's was a unique reproduction of an old California mission church with cracked plastered walls and a red tile roof. Long tables inside held fancy pyramids of semi-tropical fruit grown in Riverside labeled as products of San Bernardino County. Boxes of choice oranges and lemons had been sent to Chicago before Riverside became a county. Riverside citrus growers, including Matthew Gage, donated boxes of fruit for the agricultural display and were displeased with the San Bernardino County insignia.[12] After four weeks, the fruit displays were replaced and sold to interested parties who thought they had been grown in San Bernardino, California.

Because of Riverside's continuing unrest with San Bernardino County's Board of Supervisors, a local committee had formed to consider the formation of a new county. Accordingly, State Senator Henry Streeter, a Riverside pioneer, introduced a bill to create Riverside County. After much debate, and a special election, the bill passed the State Legislature May 9, 1893, just days after Matthew's retirement. He joined Riverside residents who celebrated formation of Riverside County with a huge bonfire on the corner of Eighth and Main streets. A local band played patriotic music as groups of young boys, with tin horns and coal oil cans, added to the music making.

Local businesses donated bales of cotton and cans of kerosene to a large contingent of young men who climbed up Rubiduox Mountain and started a roaring bonfire that was visible for miles. As Matthew watched the bright beacon, he was reminded of his two sons who had happily hiked the mountain searching for scurrying lizards and how they had played hide-and-seek among the tall boulders.

Whenever Matthew rode past Section 30, his Irish temper quickly surfaced although few souls recognized, or realized, the extent of his dilemma and indignation. He was convinced that unprincipled strangers had invaded and taken his property by virtue of a loophole in irrelevant law. The 1892 decision had renounced his ownership and resulted in victory for the claim jumpers.

In March, 1893, Matthew, through his attorneys, requested a review and revision of the cancellation of his claim to Section 30. The court, however, did not accept his proof of reclamation and cancelled his entry. This disappointing

Irrigating a Citrus Grove

decision prompted William Atwater, Jacob Gunther and Otto Newman to publish notices of their intentions of homesteading the property.

In September, the three men and their attorneys, appeared before the new Riverside County Clerk and again filed homestead entries to Section 30. Matthew showed up at the County Clerk's office at the same time and filed three contest affidavits, one for each homestead entry. He deposited $10 to pay for additional testimony, if necessary. Attorneys for the entry men objected to Matthew's presence on the grounds that he was not a party of record.[13] These demeaning banters between Gage and the entry men resulted in community gossip and conflicting opinions. The defective title and legal claim to Section 30 inched through the court system for several years. Interested citizens could not decide who should lawfully acquire the valuable property.

William Atwater began building his house on his Section 30 Homestead and Timber claim, located near Chicago Avenue. Several rows of citrus trees had been planted near the corner of Eighth Street and Canyon Crest Drive where beekeepers and hunters had trespassed. Matthew inspected the deteriorating pest house near the center of the tract and concluded that countless homeless individuals had probably found shelter there through the years. Later, on Halloween night 1899, mischievous youths or hobos set the collapsing pest house on fire.

With the severity of the 1890s depression, homeless men seeking employment had become a local and national problem. Loss of jobs had forced workers to unite as they bonded together seeking employment. In 1893, Jacob Coxey, of Massillon Ohio, became the leader of a large army of unemployed men demanding help from the United States government. Coxey announced he was leading a hundred thousand men to Washington D.C. to petition Congress to issue five million dollars of non-interest bonds for the improvement of roads to be done by unemployed men. The army traveled throughout the countryside enlisting "the unemployed" to join the march to Washington.

In the spring, Coxey's army of 50 men left Los Angeles and arrived in Arlington around noontime. The footsore, hungry gang entered the community's only grocery store and began helping themselves to any and all available food. They made coffee, cooked oatmeal, boiled rice and consumed raisins and candy and depleted the shelves. After filling their stomachs and resting awhile, they marched on to Riverside where they invaded Chinatown. Again, they helped themselves to food but cautiously only ate familiar food such as oranges and nuts. Chinese people were known to eat mysterious and strange food.

Coxey's army continued on and headed for San Bernardino. They demanded transportation to eastern states and threatened to curtail all train traffic if their demands weren't met. A railroad crew was ordered to let the men board several freight cars, take them into the desert, unhook the cars, and return to the depot.[14] Evidently Coxey's stranded army did reach Washington eventually where they protested unsuccessfully. The depression continued for several more years.

After the local invasion by Coxey's army, Matthew became concerned about his family's safety. He urged his ladies not to feed the homeless and to keep their dogs outside behind the fence. He installed an alarm bell to the barn where John could be alerted in case of an emergency. Matthew posted signs on his fences directing strangers to the Riverside Unemployment Bureau, where work and food were available from various churches. His brothers, Robert and John, visited Jane and the children when he was absent on business. After Coxey's men pillaged Arlington, citizens questioned the need of cheap Chinese labor when so many men were seeking employment.

A growing hostility against Chinese laborers became a crisis in 1893, resulting in Congress passing the Geary Chinese Exclusion Act. There were approximately 106,000 unregistered Chinese living in the United States, and those without a certificate of residence were to be deported to China. It would eliminate cheap labor and remove unsightly Chinese settlements throughout the country.

Anti-Chinese rallies were held throughout California favoring deportation. Newspapers announced: "The working people of this country are in no frame of mind to stand by and starve while Chinese are taking the bread out of their mouths."[15] After one local anti-Chinese rally, John disappeared. His meager belongings were gone and he was never heard from again. The Gages had become attached to smiling John and missed his many thoughtful acts. They prayed for his safety and wished to believe he was living with his countrymen in San Francisco.

The San Francisco-based Six Companies and various church organizations appealed to the United States Attorney General, claiming that Chinese labor was an absolute necessity to agriculture and deportation of such a large labor force would be disastrous to California's economy.

While the Chinese deportation program was generally accepted by the public, the Geary Act failed to provide sufficient funds to cover the $70 per person relocation costs to China.[16] Dozens of them were returned before deportation eventually faded away. Six Companies subsequently resumed the assignment of Chinese laborers to Riverside vineyards and citrus groves.

After several successful decades, Riverside's flourishing raisin industry began to diminish. Growers suffered low returns due to a lack of organization in marketing their fruit. An average grape farmer could realize a profit of $200 to $250 an acre under ideal conditions. As maturing navel orange groves increased, and marketing practices improved, an acre could yield as much as $1,000. Gradually vineyards were abandoned and replaced with navel orange trees and Riverside soon emerged as the orange capital of California.

Ideal climate was the leading factor in producing quality fruit. Riverside's beautiful and good-tasting fruit also required good care and an army of helpers before a grower realized any profit. The expenses of irrigation, fertilization, cultivation, frost protection and taxes had to be paid, with or without a crop. Growers, often dealing with unethical packers and shippers, took all the risks.

Several attempts had been made to improve marketing procedures before growers organized an agricultural cooperative. The first successful co-op was Riverside's Pachappa Orange Growers Association whereby growers signed binding contracts to pack and sell their fruit on a pool basis. This method evolved into the Riverside Fruit Exchange claiming:

> We do not seek to make war but dangers of haphazard marketing have to stop if the industry is to endure. We seek to offer our goods in attractive condition that will increase the demand for our fruit and open new markets. Production has passed the experimental stage and the world wants our goods. Every detail shall show care, method, and economy that pleases both producer and consumer.[17]

Matthew relied on his friends, A. J. and D. C. Twogood, to process his fruit through their packinghouse. With prospects of a systematic, regulated network, 300 growers, including Matthew and the Twogoods, initiated the Riverside Fruit Exchange. By fall, 1893, eight associations throughout southern California combined to establish the Southern California Fruit Exchange. The new organization had numerous problems due to inexperience and the deep rooted depression sweeping the country.

CHAPTER 8

During the depression years of 1893-1894, Riverside enjoyed the unique distinction of being proclaimed "the richest city in the United States in proportion to population" with the best school system in California.[1] This impressive distinction was widely publicized in an effort to promote land sales and to increase the city's population.

The *California Southern Railroad* contributed to the superlatives in an effort to lure tourists to southern California. Deluxe Pullman Palace cars, featuring upholstered spring seats, carpets and curtains and "snug" sleeping cars, ran twice daily from Riverside to Chicago.

In anticipation of a large winter tourist clientele, Frank Miller made cosmetic improvements to his Glenwood Cottage, eliminating the old tavern atmosphere and converting it into a fashionable hotel with expanded grounds. He had the south veranda enclosed in glass siding, creating a desirable sun room and added new furniture, carpeting and shaded electric lights. The Glenwood continued as a family-operated hotel and became a great Riverside asset.

Local improvements were few, however, for the nation was experiencing a serious economic depression. Several prominent Riverside businessmen became insolvent, unable to satisfy creditors. During these bleak years, Joseph Jarvis filed a petition of insolvency for $83,000 and Priestley Hall was in debt over $56,000. Regardless of these difficult times, Matthew Gage paid J. Alfonso Carit $5,500 for the note he held against his home place.[2]

The Riverside Banking Company, headed by Otis T. Dyer, foreclosed on the Rubidoux Hotel Association loan of $25,000. The bank was overextended during the prosperous boom years, with the hotel investment ultimately causing the bank's failure. Both stockholders and depositors lost money. With the advent of hard times, the prohibition question and public drunkenness surfaced once again.

THE Keeley Cure

Alcohol, Opium, Tobacco Using Produce each a disease having definite pathology. The disease yields easily to the Double Chloride of Gold Treatment as administered at the following Keeley Institutes.

Inebriety—A Disease

Inebriety, Morphine and other Drug habits are dependent upon a diseased condition of the nervous system.

The victim of the disease again and again puts forth the most heroic efforts to reform, but his disease is too absolutely overpowering to be conquered by resolutions. The will-power he would exercise if he could is no longer supreme. Alcoholic stimulants have so congested the delicate nerve cells that they cannot respond to the performance of their functional duties, and the helplessness of the victim's condition is as inexplicable to himself as it seems inexcusable to his friends.

The Keeley treatment cures this disease by restoring the nerves to a perfectly healthy state. It cures by removing the cause. The result is that the patient is left in a normal and healthy condition, and he has neither craving, desire, nor necessity for stimulants.

Over 270,000 men and women today have been permanently cured of the disease of Inebriety through Dr. Keeley's treatment, which is administered only at institutions authorized by him. The treatment at these institutions is pleasant, no restraint is imposed. It is like taking a four-weeks' vacation. He only knows he is cured.

Detailed information of this treatment, and proofs of its success, sent free upon application to any of the following institutions:

ADDRESS THE KEELEY INSTITUTE at either Hot Springs, Ark., Los Angeles, Cal., cor. North Main and Commercial Sts. West Haven, Conn. Keeley Catechism sent on application.	Washington, D. C., 905 E Street, N. W., 151 Congress St., Dwight, Ill. Marion, Ind. Kansas City, Kan., 6th St. and Ann Ave. Crab Orchard, Ky. New Orleans, La., 3507 Magazine St.	Portland, Me., Baltimore, Md., 1218 Madison Ave Lexington, Mass. Detroit, Mich., 60 Washington Ave. Minneapolis, Minn., Park Av. & 10th St. S.	Kansas City, Mo., 716 W. 10th St. St. Louis, Mo., 2803 Locust St. North Conway, N.H. Newark, N. J., 745 High St.	Buffalo, N. Y., 358 Niagara St. White Plains, N. Y. Greensboro, N. C. Cincinnati, Ohio, 451 Elm St. Columbus, Ohio, 90 N. 4th St.	Pittsburg, Pa., 4246 Fifth Ave. Providence, R. I. Greenville, S. C. Waukesha, Wis. Address the Institute nearest you.

"Non-Heredity of Inebriety," by Dr. Leslie E. Keeley, mailed upon application.

Riverside's Keeley Institute at the corner of Chestnut and Ninth Streets

The Keeley Institute, under the direction of Doctor J. P. Shumway, opened a branch office in Riverside at the corner of Ninth and Chestnut streets. The Institute rented a 16-room cottage for the treatment and cure of "liquor, opium, and cocaine habits." Doctor Leslie Keeley endorsed "the use of chloride of gold" and claimed that treatments had cured 130 graduates in six months. Dr. Keeley alleged his remedies and therapy to be highly successful, no matter how long or deeply rooted the drug problem.[3] The local institute did a thriving business despite the town's strong opposition to saloons. Congregations of 15 churches, including Calvary Presbyterian, denounced the use of alcohol, however, it is apparent not everyone was listening.

The Craft and Gage families were pillars of the Calvary Presbyterian Church where Maude and Margaret sang in the choir with their friend, Marcia Craft. Margaret Gage had a delightful soprano voice, but Marcia's singing was recognized as extraordinary. Marcia gave serious attention to her musical studies and hoped to become a talented soloist. Each Sunday, she delighted the congregation with her melodious renderings and became a special sweetheart to church members.

When Marcia graduated from Riverside High School in June 1893, Reverend George H. Deere of the First Universalist Church presented her diploma stating: "May your life be a song, so sweet and true that it shall join at last in harmony with the Angel above."[4]

Matthew and Jane encouraged Marcia's father, Hiram Craft, to allow his daughter to seriously study music with an accomplished maestro. After several attempts failed to raise funds for a professional teacher, local businessmen loaned Marcia $1,200 to study in Boston. Due to hard times and the increasing number of organizations seeking funds, some donors remained anonymous, including Matthew Gage. Matthew's daughter Maude corresponded with her girlfriend, who, in time, became an international diva, known as Marcella Craft, one of Riverside's most famous personalities.[5]

Matthew became even more critical of the Trust Company when it offered to extend the Gage Canal to irrigate lands of the San Jacinto Tin Company. The English-owned company had ceased business in 1892 when the tin market collapsed. Subsequently reorganized as the San Jacinto Land Company, it planned to develop the acreage into citrus groves, following water negotiations with the Trust Company.

Matthew Gage had no control over the policies or services of the Gage Canal after selling his interests to the Trust Company. Nevertheless, he voiced his concerns that extending the canal would result in less water for existing stockholders and inevitably increase future assessments. He contended that development of the San Jacinto Land Company would be in direct competition with future sales in Arlington Heights.

At this time, Matthew had little income. Jane mortgaged My Sweet Anna, then in her name, and gave the money to Matthew. In return, he conveyed his water rights to canal water to his wife, as security for the loan. This agreement, transacted in the fall of 1893 between husband and wife, included an option allowing him to recover his water stock whenever necessary.

After Matthew resigned as manager of the Trust Company, he turned his attention to the complex ownership of Section 30. He decided to research United States land laws and to pursue his claim through the highest courts. In October 1893, he moved to Washington D.C. to consult with government officials. Jane supported her husband's mission and stood by his decisions.

After Gage's Chinese John disappeared, the family hired Jose and Maria, a hardworking married couple. They lived in the enlarged carriage house and became devoted to the family. Jose maintained the grounds and grove and Maria assisted Jane with household chores. Matthew had faith in his family's safety with Jose and Maria living on the property.

In July 1894, during one of his infrequent visits to Riverside, he met with his attorneys, William Collier and Lyman Evans, to prepare legal documents for an anticipated lawsuit against the Riverside Trust Company, Limited, and the Northern Counties Investment Trust Company, Limited. During his stay in Washington D.C. researching laws pertaining to Section 30, he instructed his Riverside attorneys to file papers and begin proceedings upon receipt of his telegram to that effect. When negotiations with the two English-based companies failed, Collier & Evans received the telegram and on August 24, 1894, they filed suit on behalf of Matthew Gage.

The complaint alleged that between March 1890 and March 1891, the Trust Company sold 936 acres with water rights in Arlington Heights for $446,000. After payment of all expenses, interest and dividends, records revealed a $200,000 profit. Gage contended that his A and B-shares in the Trust Company should have returned enough money to liquidate his indebtedness to the company. This included his $40,000 purchase of 60 acres in Arlington Heights near Victoria Avenue and Jane Street. When the Trust Company declared "no profits forthcoming," the financial statements, and accounting records, could not be located and were declared missing. Matthew accused the company of fraud and of falsifying documents.[6]

In addition, Matthew claimed that he had been misinformed and deceived concerning terms of the original Trust Company purchase, including promised benefits due him. Gage expected his B-shares to produce cash dividends with the sale of Arlington Heights land. The company, however, changed its plans and retained the property, planting it with citrus groves. Consequently, in order to raise essential capital, Gage negotiated a personal loan through Wilson Crewdson, whereby he relinquished his B-shares in the Trust Company and borrowed approximately $290,000 to buy higher yielding A-shares.

On an undisclosed date, Crewdson assigned Matthew's note to the Northern Counties Investment Trust Company, Limited, a corporation comprised of directors on the board of the Trust Company. Gage claimed the Northern Counties Company could have collected money due them from the Trust Company, where his pledged shares were worth $750,000.

Matthew identified the two companies as indistinguishable, with the president of the Northern Counties owning 860 A-shares in the Trust Company. Matthew accused the Northern Counties Trust of defrauding him of funds due him from the Riverside Trust Company and requested a $500,000 judgment.

Court records later revealed that Matthew Gage had not paid any interest on his Northern Counties note in three years. According to the company, "Mr. Gage held no further interest in the assigned entitlements, or contracts, and the matter is closed."[7] Unfortunately, Matthew received nothing in return for his endeavors to regain what he believed to be his rightful, legitimate benefits. Matthew Gage's association with the canal he had built and Arlington Heights properties ended in 1894.

John Greenleaf North had a strong bent for the law and in 1894 passed the California bar examination and opened his law office in Riverside. He became the recognized authority on irrigation and water rights law as a result of his many years as superintendent and president of the Riverside Water Company.

John G. North

Because of his expertise, the Riverside Trust Company and their allied corporations hired him to oversee their Riverside investments.[8] Matthew Gage and John G. North, both unyielding in their opinions and deliberations, were destined to clash, both inside and outside courtrooms.

There were tight-lipped accusations of fraud, deceit and double-dealing on the part of the Riverside Trust Company. There were reservations as to Matthew's dubious business practices and his headstrong optimism. Gossipmongers had a field day taking sides as to who was the righteous party when Matthew sued the Trust Company. Bizarre behavior of the English directors and Matthew Gage has been debated for decades by friends, relatives and enemies. Justification for these actions, by both parties, has fortunately been obliterated with the passage of time.

After living in Washington D.C., and frequent trips to England, Matthew returned to Riverside in April 1895. Later that year, three separate motions, disputing title to Section 30, were filed with the Riverside County Records Office. William E. Atwater, Jacob J. Gunther, and Otto H. Newman gave legal notice:

> To all persons dealing with said Matthew Gage in regard to said land, that in case he shall procure receiver's certificates of final payment for said lands, or any part thereof, or shall receive government patents for the said lands, or any part thereof, they will take such legal proceedings as may be necessary to charge said Matthew Gage as holder of the title of said lands as their trustee and to compel the transfer of the title to the same to them by all proper conveyances.[9]

Matthew took legal action, asking the court to re-review the case decided against him in 1892. Title disputes relating to this valuable section of land had been ongoing for nine years. With delays and more delays the case for review and appeal finally took place on September 26, 1895.

Matthew traveled to Washington D. C. where the Department of the Interior, General Land Office, considered his petition for a review of the case. There were voluminous documents pertaining to decisions that had cancelled Matthew's Desert Land entry. Days of testimony, open discussions, and debatable facts kept attorneys busy on both sides. Local newspapers reported:

> Secretary of the Interior, Hoke Smith finally concluded: It seems to me the first years of Gage's entry were spent by him in efforts to obtain a sufficient water supply by a system of artesian wells upon which he expended a large sum of money. When this plan proved impracticable, he turned his efforts to other methods of obtaining water.

He finally succeeded in obtaining an abundant supply from the Santa Ana River, 12-miles from his land. This appears to be the nearest available water to be obtained. He expended upward of $300,000 in the purchase of water right-of-way and construction of his canal, reaching the land with an abundant supply of water, after the three years expired, but before any adverse claim had intervened.

We must observe the rules but from a view of the whole case, a just conclusion has not yet been reached. Justice to both parties will be secured by reopening said case. Therefore, it's directed that Gage be allowed final proof before the Board of Equitable Adjudication. Homestead entries 673-4-5 stand suspended.[10]

Riverside newspapers printed detailed articles about the case, stating more litigation was promised as Matthew Gage continued fighting for Section 30. *The Riverside Daily Press* stated:

The contestants claimed a right to file on the ground he had failed to put water upon it in the time required by law. Mr. Gage claimed the parties who jumped it were the ones employed to do the work upon the canal and the delay was due to their desire to take advantage of him. He is now a comparatively poor man.

Meanwhile the increasing number of newly planted citrus groves had produced a need for additional packinghouses. By the 1894-1895 season, there were 12 local packing companies. Each house hired pickers, generally Japanese men, who received three to three-and a-half cents a box, and were capable of earning $2.50 to $4 a day.[11] The majority of Chinese laborers had left town when the government attempted to enforce the Geary Exclusion Act. Jose cared for Matthew's home grove of ten acres and proceeds from the navel orange crop supported the family. Matthew, eager to plant Section 30, envisioned future prosperity from hundreds of acres of orange groves.

Before he could begin to improve his property, however, Atwater and associates again filed a protest against his title. This unexpected action incurred additional lengthy legal delays. The protesters, however, gained enough time to harvest several more crops of alfalfa from Section 30.

During Matthew's absence from Riverside, William Irving had designed a three-story house, and elegant carriage house, to be erected in Arlington Heights for his large family. His son, William Gage Irving, a student in the law office of Purington & Adair, passed the law examination in Los Angeles and in 1896 was admitted to the bar. The Irving residence on Fourteenth Street had been an adequate residence, but, as manager of the Trust Company, it seemed appropriate that he live on the Heights. In 1895, he chose a superb 20 acre site, east of Victoria Avenue on Maude Street, above the Gage Canal. The following year, he built his house on a knoll that offered a spectacular view. With the help of his brother-in-law, Robert Gage, he designed a redwood mansion, incorporating many of his original architectural ideas.

The Trust Company encouraged his endeavor, considering it an endorsement of future stately mansions. Several notable Englishmen had established substantial homes in Arlington Heights and William Irving's was a welcome addition. When contractor D. J. McLeod completed the house the following year, Irving named his family home, Raeburn, in honor of his birthplace in Scotland.[12] The impressive 7,400-square-foot house, with its stately entry hall and seven bedrooms, became a noted Riverside landmark. Matthew and his family joined the Irvings to celebrate the completion of Raeburn, the first of many family gatherings held in the house during the ensuing years. It became a pleasant custom for relatives to assemble in Raeburn for afternoon tea, served in the comfortable atmosphere of the country estate.

Raeburn, Residence of the Irving family, 1898

In March 1896, the *San Francisco Chronicle* published an important news item:

GAGE VICTORY
Secretary of the Interior holds in Gage's favor against Homesteaders. Gage appealed to the Secretary of the Interior and the case was appealed to the Board of Equitable Adjudication which body decided Gage had rights in the case and granted him permission to perfect his entry. This decision was appealed to the Secretary of the Interior by Atwater and associates in form of protest against Gage perfecting his title. This protest was overruled by Secretary of the Interior who ordered a Patent to be issued to Gage. Once in possession of the Patent, no courts can deprive Gage of his title unless it can be shown such Patent was fraudulently obtained.

On April 21, 1896, in the Superior Court, County of Riverside, California, a patent was issued decreeing:

> Matthew Gage absolute owner entitled to possession of all the land embraced in Section 30. Section Thirty in Township two south of Range Four west of San Bernardino Meridian in California containing six-hundred thirty-seven acres and sixty-one-hundredths of an acre. In testimony hereof, I, Grover Cleveland, President of the United States Of America, have caused these letters to be made Patent, and the seal of The General Land Office to be hereunto affixed.

Gage's victory was acknowledged throughout California as citizens rejoiced for his good fortune. Matthew leased several acres in Section 30 to dry farmers, even though Atwater and his cohorts remained on the land. The ongoing battle was far from terminated.

English speaking people around the world united in June 1897 to honor good Queen Victoria on the occasion of her Diamond Jubilee. For 60 years, 78-year-old Queen Victoria had ruled Great Britain and Ireland and served as Empress of India. Her Jubilee became an international festival and Riverside joined

Queen Victoria's Diamond Jubilee 1897

133

in the celebration with an elaborate presentation in the Loring Opera House. Loyal subjects and other admirers filled the magnificently decorated theater.

Three becoming portraits of her Majesty, with Union Jack flags draped around each frame, stood on the stage covered in flowers. Next to the Queen's likeness were several portraits of President William McKinley draped in American flags. Distinguished citizens including Matthew Gage, John Jarvis and Frank Miller, were honorably recognized, and seated upon the stage.

A variety of performers entertained the jovial crowd with sentimental music and amusing poetry recitations. Everyone joined the happy community sing-a-long and the evening was filled with laughter and good fellowship. The master of ceremonies, George Frost, read a community telegram sent to the good Queen:

> The citizens of Riverside, California, British born and American, send greetings on this the sixtieth anniversary of Your Majesty's Coronation, which we celebrate. God Save The Queen.
> Signed, Mayor Edward Kingman.[13]

The tribute to Queen Victoria was long remembered as one of the town's grandest celebrations with nothing lacking, an appropriate and fitting gala.

A few months later, in August, another illustrious celebration took place in Riverside. The United States Congress passed the Dingley Bill at an opportune time to save the orange industry from destruction. The new tariff required foreign growers to pay 70 cents per box, instead of 20 cents, for the privilege of selling their fruit in American markets. Passage of this bill equalized prices for California and foreign grown oranges in eastern markets. California growers were paying 90 cents per box for freight to New York.

The Los Angeles Chamber of Commerce, with Colonel Harrison Gray Otis of the *Los Angeles Times*, had contributed thousands of dollars to pass a fair tariff bill and Riverside celebrated the occasion along with other communities in southern California. The Riverside Band paraded through downtown streets and fireworks brightened the skyline. Jubilee colors of green and yellow were displayed everywhere, especially in the Glenwood Hotel.

That evening a lavish banquet at the Glenwood began at 10 o'clock with electric lights in the decorated dining room spelling "Long Life To Our Friends." Ohlmyer's orchestra played popular tunes of the day. Guests indulged in soup, salmon, and fillet of beef, potatoes, chicken, asparagus and Tariff Punch. At the end of the evening, guests lifted their glasses, filled with non-alcoholic punch, and toasted the Government of the United States for passing the tariff bill.[14] Matthew and his fellow growers eagerly anticipated higher fruit returns.

The fruit growers in Arlington Heights were encouraged with the prospect of receiving better citrus returns. After William Irving moved into his lovely home, he invited several prominent citrus growers and a reporter from the *Riverside Daily Press* to tour his property and to inspect the successful co-operative pumping plant installed in the arroyo near his house. Gage Canal water from below his house was conveyed through an eight-inch pipe by a 20-horsepower electric motor to property above the canal. The age of electricity improved irrigation practices when land above gravity flow canals could be irrigated. Electric pumps furnished water to thousands of acres of otherwise useless land. Irving's home electric plant serviced 89 acres, including the groves of three neighbors.

William Irving drove his guests through Arlington Heights. He commented that it was important for friends and neighbors to know one another and that he hoped Riversiders had learned that "we cannot live to ourselves." He believed, "An individual cannot be successful unless the community in which he lives is successful." The dignified gentleman managed Arlington Heights without incident for seven years and was a respected community leader. In 1898, he became

Gravity flow no longer necessary with gas or electric irrigation pumps.

an American citizen after passage of the federal Sherman Antitrust Act of 1890 that "forbid combinations of foreign trusts, or any attempt to monopolize commerce, as opposed to the American system of free enterprise." The Riverside Trust Company incorporated several citrus-related companies to extend their services to Arlington Heights growers and to comply with the law.[15]

Matthew Gage's comings and goings were no longer considered newsworthy as he often traveled to England to redeem stock in the Trust Company or to Washington D.C. to examine government land laws. In October 1897, he sold 14 inches of unattached water stock in the Gage Canal to A. J. Twogood for $12,000. The next day he left for San Francisco, presumably to settle other outstanding loans. Business, however, did not prevent his participation in happy family events like the one described in the *Riverside Press*:

> About one of the prettiest weddings that Riverside has seen in many a day took place at noon on May 25, 1898 when Elizabeth Brow Irving, eldest daughter of Mr. and Mrs. William Irving, and John Malloch Mylne were united in Calvary Presbyterian Church. The bride wore white silk with a traditional bridal veil and carried a bouquet of white carnations. Maids of honor, in Kate Greenway costumes of white silk, included Kathleen Irving, Maude Gage, and Margaret Gage. The ceremony was performed by Reverend Arnold and assisted by Reverend Solomon Mylne, father of the groom. The wedding party repaired to Raeburn where a wedding lunch was served and the newlyweds received congratulations of friends and relatives.[16]

Two weeks later, another family wedding took place at Calvary Church at high noon when Janie Gage, eldest daughter of Robert Gage, married Doctor T. H. Farrell of Utica, New York. The bride wore a beautiful gown of white satin and a conventional wedding veil. Maude served as maid of honor for her cousin, who would soon leave for Utica where her husband enjoyed a lucrative medical practice.[17] In spite of Matthew Gage's personal problems, and the gravity of his lawsuits, he rejoiced at his nieces' weddings and wished them many years of blissful marriage.

A professor at Yale predicted that the world would end in 1899, primarily from lack of water.[18] Matthew knew capped wells in the Victoria Tract would provide water for a long period of time and dismissed the forecast. His immediate problem concerned Section 30, where entry men now claimed that Matthew's patent for Section 30, issued by the United States government, conveyed no title. In defiance of the 1896 patent, William Atwater and family continued to live in their small, frame house located on Section 30. In 1897, he planted 60 acres of alfalfa, and harvested one ton of hay per acre. After he planted dozens of small eucalyptus trees bordering Eighth Street, a band of sheep were herded down that road on their way to Box Springs and the community of Alessandro. The sheep left the road in search of food, trampling and killing Atwater's young trees.[19]

Section 30 continued to be thought of as a public domain and Matthew was determined to resolve the problem through legal action to rid the property of squatters like Atwater. After conferring with his attorney, papers were filed and he was advised not to encounter or assault any intruders or occupants on his land while legal actions were pending. Continuing legal obstacles delayed his case against Atwater, Gunther and Newman for more than a year, until May 1899, when Judge Joseph S. Noyes, presiding Judge of the Superior Court of Riverside County, handed down a decision vital to Matthew Gage.

CHAPTER 9

When Matthew took action to eject Atwater, Gunther and Newman from Section 30, they, in turn, filed a cross complaint. This resulted in a hotly contested suit, costing thousands of dollars. When proceedings began in April 1899, friends and relatives of both parties filled Judge Joseph S. Noyes' Superior Courtroom located in the Arlington Hotel. Riverside County rented space for governmental offices in the eight-year-old, three-story building located on the northwest corner of Lime and Eighth streets. The impressive hotel, considered the grandest in Riverside, featured corner towers and banks of bay windows, and housed the only elevator in town.[1]

Matthew, Jane, and William Irving, attended daily proceedings and were encouraged to have friends and acquaintances in the courtroom. Joseph and John Jarvis, James

Arlington Hotel, Eighth and Lime Streets

Roe, A. J. Twogood and Frank Miller appeared periodically in the crowded courtroom, filled to capacity each day.

Garber & Garber, attorneys from San Francisco, and William Gage Irving, Matthew's nephew, represented Matthew Gage, the plaintiff, in his request to regain possession of Section 30, awarded him in 1896 by the Department of the Interior. Atwater, Gunther, and Newman, the defendants, were represented by R. E. Houghton of San Francisco, who challenged Gage's title to Section 30, claiming fraudulent representation in the United States patent issued to Matthew Gage.

Judge Noyes reviewed previous proceedings, and propositions of law, for the benefit of the court reporter and his records.

> The issues involved in this action are purely questions of law with the simple exception of the one alleging fraud. The land, the title of which is the bone of contention between parties embraces all of Section 30. Originally located by Matthew Gage in 1882 under the Desert Land Act and subsequently entered and located by defendants in 1886 under the Homestead and Timber Acts. Since its original location by Gage, the larger part of the tract has been incorporated within territorial limits of the City of Riverside. From its worthless nature as desert land, when first located in 1882, it has increased in value conservatively estimated not less than $150,000 to $200,000.

> Under plaintiff's failure to conduct water upon the land within the three years prescribed by law, defendants instigated contests for their respected portions of the same in the Land Department. The defendants claim the Secretary of the Interior, and other officials of the Land Office, misinterpreted and misapplied the law granting Matthew Gage the Patent. They also contend

Gage and department officials committed fraud in the procurement and granting of the Patent.

After Gage's first hearing before Secretary of the Interior, and the decision against his claim, he petitioned for a review, a rehearing, and Secretary Smith referred the matter to the Board of Equitable Adjudication to ascertain Gage's rights. Rights of the defendants were not denied or compromised.[2]

The defendant's first issue had to do with title to the land. Consequently Mr. Houghton attempted to prove the land unsuitable to have qualified under the Desert Land Act and, therefore, deemed it subject to cancellation. William Atwater testified he first knew of Section 30 in 1882 when he crossed the property to hunt on Box Springs Mountain. He remembered seeing squatters, Austin and Keeney, who had cultivated a patch of alfalfa on the land. He also recalled a man named French, who planted 10 acres of barley on the northwest corner of Section 30. Atwater considered that this cultivated land proved Section 30 did not qualify as desert land.

Photographs were presented as positive evidence that the land in question did not qualify as desert land and did qualify as homestead land. Mr. Houghton had ordered Perry S. Corl, a professional photographer, to take photos of William Atwater's house on Section 30. The picture depicted a large, two-storied, four-gabled house, barely visible behind an orchard of fruit trees. Identification across the bottom read:

Residence of W. A. Atwater on homestead claim. Fruit trees and shade trees about the house on land claimed by Gage to be valueless for homesteads and so found in decision of September 26, 1895.[3]

The house, mislabeled as Atwater's house, belonged to Otto Lowentrout and was located across the street on

Mysterious Photo Number 57

the southwest corner of Eighth Street and Chicago Avenue. Matthew testified his first knowledge of the existence of photograph number 57 was when he found it misfiled among documents in the Department of the Interior in Washington D. C. In reality, Atwater had a three-room house, valued at $400, with a sawed shake shingle roof and little vegetation nearby.

When this perverted evidence was brought to the attention of the court, no one knew who was responsible for the identifying words at the bottom of the photograph. The defendants said Corl, the photographer, was to blame for not getting the correct angle to view Atwater's house. Muffled sounds could be heard throughout the courtroom as no one could offer a rational explanation as to how Lowentrout's house could be mistaken for Atwater's house.

In response to Mr. Houghton's convincing argument that Section 30 produced vegetation without water, and therefore did not qualify as desert land, Matthew's attorneys called upon three prominent citizens. The first, Stephen Herrick, owner of considerable nearby property, testified that he could not recollect crops of any value ever having grown on Section 30. Other property owners, Priestley Hall and John Jarvis, reported that the land had long been useless without water. At the end of their testimony, a polite, soft applause of approval by spectators could be heard throughout the courtroom.

The defendants next line of attack alleged Section 30 could not be irrigated from said canal and that water had not been delivered to 175 acres on the southeast corner above Gage's canal. Mr. Houghton, Atwater's attorney stressed that water had not been applied upon the land sufficiently to reclaim or irrigate it. He therefore concluded that Gage was in non-compliance with provisions of the Desert Land Act.

Gage's attorney refuted this argument and maintained that he had applied water upon the land, as decisions of previous cases had proved. William G. Irving declared, "Reclamation is an accomplished fact where the water in sufficient volume is brought on the land and so disposed as to render it valuable when needed." He furthermore stated that Matthew Gage had put water upon the land and, with the aid of additional ditches, permitted water to flow and cover most of Section 30. By applying water, the entire section benefited, and Mr. Irving insisted Matthew Gage had complied with the law, and fulfilled every requirement of the law, "both in letter and spirit."

The third argument from the defense had to do with the time period for reclamation. The law prescribed a three-year period for Desert Land and Gage had taken four years. At the conclusion of three years, in January 1886, William Atwater and associates filed Homestead affidavits with the Commissioner of General Land Office for portions of Section 30, believing it open for contest. Mr. Houghton maintained officials of the Land Department misinterpreted and misapplied the law granting Gage the patent. Furthermore, he believed Gage and department officials committed fraud in procurement and granting of the patent.

In response, Matthew's attorney claimed that he had acted in good faith and "with increasing diligence" to complete the canal. "There were adverse obstacles thrown in his way by adverse claimants and unforeseen natural barriers and unnecessary delays."[4]

After more than a month of citing United States statutes, rulings and regulations and arguments, Judge Noyes handed down his findings on May 29, 1899:

> There is no question but that Gage acted in good faith and with unceasing diligence in his efforts to reclaim Section 30. It is apparent to the court that through the ignorance, or mistake, of his engineers, their miscalculation as to the time required to construct the canal and the obstacles thrown in his way by adverse claimants, as well as by natural barriers, not contemplated at the threshold of his undertaking, prevented a literal compliance with the law but under both principle and authority he has by his honesty of intention and perseverance brought himself within the well-established rules of justice.
>
> I find no question of law presented meriting serious consideration as to whether Gage has been guilty of fraud in procuring his Patent. The charges of fraud made by the defendants are but allegations of irregularities which in no way jeopardize the rights of the defendants or operated as a deception on the government. No rights to defendants were compromised or denied. The ruling of this court finds that no fraud was practiced by Gage nor of the Land Department.
>
> The evidence is insufficient to justify or sustain additional finding that the defendants entered into possession of the premises described in the complaint without right or title, and they wrongly withhold the possession of the same from the plaintiff. The Secretary of the Interior and the Board of Equitable Adjudication wisely decided that Gage was right and should be granted a Patent, and this court gladly extends its aiding hand to confirm their mandate.
>
> J.S. Noyes, Judge

Matthew and his family were relieved to have the ownership of Section 30 finally settled, once and for all. He had been under a great deal of stress for a number of years battling over the controversy of this land. Despite this successful conclusion, however, another hotly contested suit emerged while Judge Noyes was hearing the trial of Gage vs. Atwater, etc. In August, the Riverside Trust Company, Limited, brought charges against Mr. Gage in regard to ownership of acreage that he purchased in Arlington Heights in 1891.[5] Matthew's life now seemed consumed by legal proceedings, a dismal and exhausting existence. The need for religious faith and spiritual support became apparent during Matthew's months of frustrations.

Before his case against Atwater and associates began he had found little time to devote to his Calvary Church activities. When he turned to his pastor for spiritual guidance he received little comfort. One Sunday in April, Reverend W. F. Arnold of the Calvary Presbyterian Church announced his leave of absence due to health problems. He asked the congregation to attend the coming week's prayer meeting and requested a full attendance. Matthew, Jane and the girls attended Thursday services and both the lecture room and ladies' parlor were filled to capacity.

Reverend W. F. Arnold
Calvary Presbyterian Church

After devotional exercises, Pastor Arnold reviewed his two-year ministry in Riverside and his attempts to bring prayer meetings up to his ideals. He deplored his failure and asked the audience, "Why is this great attendance not always the rule?" He emphasized prayer meetings should be a place of prayer and confidence and questioned why it had not been. He said, "Presbyterians as a rule are conservative, however, Calvary Presbyterian Church is the most conservative of conservatives."[6] He had little assistance from his congregation and referred to the silence of his elders in prayer meetings and their frequent absence from meetings. The crowded assembly was stunned into silence and Matthew regretted that he had not been more involved in his church's activities.

Robert Gage, a church elder, assured Pastor Arnold that "neither silence nor absence on part of the elders, or others of his flock, reflected lack of love or admiration for him." He affirmed that his ministry of two years had been a blessing to Calvary Church and wished him a speedy restoration of health and faith on his holiday from the church. Pastor Arnold had arranged an amiable exchange with his brother who was in charge of a large church in Cleveland, Ohio. The congregation wished him God speed and awaited his return in the fall. Unfortunately, Reverend Arnold passed away shortly after leaving Riverside. Matthew Gage came to the realization that his problems could only be solved by his own due diligence and his deep faith in his church teachings.

Two days after Matthew's Section 30 victory, the case of Jarvis vs. the Riverside Trust Company commenced in the Superior Court of Judge York.[7] Dr. Joseph Jarvis was suing the Trust Company for $10,000, alleging that they harvested lemon and orange crops on land he leased from Matthew Gage. The case had been postponed in April, pending the Riverside Trust Company's suit against Matthew Gage. The decision of the Jarvis case would have material bearing upon the first case. Judge York decided it was best to wait for a definite decision and returned the case to the docket to be rescheduled. A confused public could not easily unravel

Gage's legal proceedings that were often linked together in concurrent lawsuits.

During the summer months, Gage relatives gathered at Raeburn to play golf on a short, dirt course located behind the house and later everyone gathered for tea. With the families of Robert Gage, William John, Matthew Gage, and William Irving, it was a large assembly of congenial relatives. These family gatherings were pleasant encounters for Matthew, an escape from ongoing problems and contentious courtrooms. William Irving's house was surrounded by a variety of trees planted and maintained by Franz Hosp who had developed a small nursery on the property.[8] There he nurtured shrubs, flowers, and decorative trees, such as eucalyptus, palm and pepper, to be planted throughout Arlington Heights.

In August, Matthew Gage was again in Judge Noyes' Superior Court. This time it involved a counterclaim against the Riverside Trust Company, Limited, that had filed a foreclosure suit against him the previous year. The Trust Company asserted that he had not made principal payments on the $40,000 purchase price, or interest, on 60 acres that he had contracted to purchase in 1891. This case was carefully followed because of its important interpretations of law and equity.

Judge Noyes reviewed previous proceedings dating back to 1898 when the Trust Company filed a foreclosure suit against Gage. In defense, Gage filed a counterclaim and the trial between a prosperous English corporation and an unyielding, stubborn Irishman shook the town.

After weeks of testimony from reliable witnesses and lengthy explanations on points of law, Judge Noyes handed down his decision on August 26, 1899.[9]

> I will simply present in an abbreviated way my reasons in deciding issues in this case. The defendant, Gage claims damages in the sum of $20,000 for failure to supply water to the land in question. I am satisfied the defendant was not in fault for this failure and

reliable witnesses attribute damages to the loss of crops aggregate to $45,000 less deductions. I am of the opinion that the $20,000 claim is nearly correct and must be allowed.

The defendant agrees to pay the taxes on the land and I believe that inequity and good conscience this contention should be maintained. The case of title has to do with the lien and complicated points of law. The land would necessarily be taxed to the mortgagee, holding legal title however, Matthew Gage paid all taxes. The contract to pay all taxes on the land is an agreement to pay taxes on all of the interest of the mortgage. I am satisfied that the issue here has never been fully presented to the Supreme Court upon its merits.

The contention of the defendant as to compensation to Gage should account for the water rates and assessments assessed on the land, but not required to pay for work done on the land.

Judge J. S. Noyes

Matthew was relieved to have access to Block 65 and to be paid punitive damages. To celebrate the conclusion of another trial, Matthew and Jane attended a festive trolley party. The *Riverside & Arlington Railroad*, managed by Frank Miller, had retired the mules once used to pull the cars. Electric wires for trolley operation installed in 1899 ran from First and Main streets to Magnolia Avenue and continued on Magnolia to Van Buren Boulevard. Several trolley cars transported passengers and a deluxe parlor car was often used for parties.[10]

The Gages joined Calvary Presbyterian Church friends for a September party in an open trolley car, cheerfully decorated in red, white, and blue. Bunting was attached to the front and rear of the car and small electric lights glowed inside. The conductor rang a bell, signaling the motorman to

Riverside's Electric Trolley Car

start the seven mile journey. During the leisurely ride to Van Buren Boulevard, passengers sang their favorite tunes along Magnolia Avenue. Matthew remembered his second day in Riverside, riding down the Avenue to visit his orange grove for the first time. The town had grown from a small colony to an expanding city and he wondered how much his canal had contributed to such growth.

Frank Miller was at the helm of the local street car system, considered a major asset to the community. Tourists viewed the landscape from the electric streetcars where they could ride from downtown to Arlington in half an hour.[11] There were infrequent occasions when streetcars became moving vans with furniture and household items piled aboard to be transported from one place to another.

In the fall of 1899, attorneys for Atwater, Gunther and Newman and Matthew Gage were summoned to Judge Noyes' chambers to settle the recording judgment in the case of Section 30: "Matthew Gage is the absolute owner and holds title to real properties described as Section 30."[12] In reality, however, the fight was not over.

Shortly after Section 30 was finally recorded, Matthew received word from Miss Dolph, a church volunteer, that Mr. and Mrs. Atwater requested an interview with him. She indicated that the Atwaters were sick and tired of fighting and wanted to terminate their claim to Section 30. They met in the home of Reverend George Lyman, a retired minister who lived on the corner of Main and Fifteenth streets. During their conference, Mr. and Mrs. Atwater gave Matthew a quit claim deed to property in Section 30, and said they would vacate as soon as possible.[13] Despite Atwater's withdrawal, Gunther and Newman remained on Section 30. Subsequently, the Atwater family moved to Pasadena.

The Atwaters confided to Matthew that Mr. Houghton had taken their case with the understanding that he would benefit from their acquisition. However, Gunther and Newman had lost confidence in his counsel after his threats of civil proceedings and had instigated a movement for a substitution of attorney. Mr. Houghton then claimed he had a contract with the three men to fight the case to a finish on a contingent fee. It was his intention to appeal and he implied they had no legal right to change lawyers.

Matthew Gage's Irish temper ignited over Houghton's disrespect for the court, and his previous attempt to deceive the Secretary of the Interior in presenting false photographs labeled as Atwater's house. He grew furious when he heard of threats to the families who wanted a new attorney to represent them. Matthew filed a suit to disbar R. E. Houghton of San Francisco.[14] His Riverside friends tried to dissuade him, asserting such a trial would be complicated and futile. At the time, Matthew Gage was still being sued by the Trust Company. After filing papers on August 14, 1899, the case was not heard until the following spring.

Ethan Allen Chase, of the firm Chase Brothers of Rochester, New York, purchased considerable acreage around

Riverside in the 1890s. He had been the head of one of the largest nurseries in the United States and his decision to settle in Riverside displayed his confidence in the community and its potential of producing good-tasting navel oranges. Chase and his sons Martin, Harry and Frank, eventually became the largest individual growers in the area, respected local businessmen and civic leaders.[15] Matthew befriended the Chase family and introduced them to the Calvary Presbyterian Church, where they became faithful members.

Robert Henderson, representing eastern fruit shippers, visited Riverside in 1897 and decided to move his family west. He purchased Lot 2, Block 12 in Arlington Heights from the Riverside Trust Company. His 10 acres of five-year-old citrus trees offered a hillside building site with a panoramic view of the distant mountains and valley. The Henderson family of New York, included Robert, his wife Jennet, then daughter Jean, and sons, Robert, Henry and William. Mrs. Henderson and Jean lived in the Glenwood Hotel for several months where they worked with Robert Gage in designing their future hillside home.[16]

During the summer of 1899, a rumbling noise swept through town as Riverside experienced an earthquake. The first jolt, in the morning, startled everyone and a stronger shock around noon quickly emptied all county offices and courtrooms in the Arlington Hotel. Many residents ran into the streets to avoid falling debris as after shocks continued throughout the day and night. The disturbance, centered in the San Bernardino Mountains, produced landslides and trapped miners in damaged tunnels.[17]

Merchandise was thrown from shelves in local stores. Cracked plaster walls were common and shattered glass was everywhere. The following day many more sharp jolts occurred and recent new residents wondered if they really wanted to live in such an unpredictable region. After the quakes subsided, citizens noticed an increased flow of water in streams, wells and rivers. The Gages had experienced previous earthquakes but their new friends, the Robert

Henderson and Ethan Allen Chase families from New York, were apprehensive about such geological events.

Five months later, at 4 o'clock Christmas morning, the town was awakened by a stronger shake. The most severe jolts damaged the nearby towns of Hemet and San Jacinto, destroying all brick buildings. Chimneys cracked, bottles broke, and adobe buildings collapsed. Pianos moved, clocks stopped, and china and furniture were ruined. The twisting motion of the quake crumbled south-facing walls. Christmas church services were quickly cancelled and people kept outdoors as small jolts continued for several days. Jose and Maria felt unsafe living in the old Gage carriage house.

Gloom and dejection faced residents of the hard hit towns. Merchants were forced to guard their merchandise day and night. They used lanterns to ward off night prowlers and questioned the presence of inquisitive tourists.[18] Small earthquakes continued and the curious and eccentric arrived on special trains to see the destruction in San Jacinto and Hemet. Photographs of demolished homes and buildings were produced on postcards and rapidly sold in shops throughout southern California. This earthquake was considered California's most destructive since the great 1821 quake.

On January 1, 1900, another strong earthquake hit, moving east to west, much like the Christmas morning quake. No one wanted to begin the new century with an earthquake of any magnitude. With a resigned attitude the *Riverside Daily Press* commented, "We enter upon a New Year, and a new Century, with new problems to face."

CHAPTER 10

On Thursday March 1, 1900, Matthew Gage, plaintiff, filed papers in the Riverside County Clerk's Office to disbar R. E. Houghton, the defendant, a well-known San Francisco attorney and judge. The action against Mr. Houghton had begun in August 1899, but due to numerous motions, hearings had been postponed many times. Matthew Gage had requested one delay in order to attend a business meeting in London and another delay was due to the judge's illness.

The celebrated case was held in the Superior Court of Riverside County with Judge Hughes of San Diego presiding. Matthew's attorney, Mr. Aird A. Adair of Riverside, was a personal friend from Ontario, Canada, who belonged to the Calvary Presbyterian Church. The 43-year-old solicitor had moved to town in 1890 and formed a partnership with W. A. Purington, establishing a prominent, respected firm.[1]

Gage alleged that Mr. Houghton prepared several land affidavits that he knew to be false. Charges involved photographs given in evidence in the fall of 1895 to deceive the Secretary of the Interior, Hoke Smith. One photo, Exhibit 57, was labeled "W. A. Atwater's residence with improvements," when he knew the picture was, in reality, the house and grounds of Otto A. Lowentrout. Gage contended that Mr. Houghton had attempted to mislead the Honorable Court. Matthew Gage claimed that Houghton's actions were unjust, immoral, and dishonorable and that they perverted his duty as a counselor and attorney.

Defendant Houghton asserted Gage's object in the proceedings was revenge for alleged derogatory assertions in the courts for nearly 20 years. Houghton was confident that he was the only person who could defeat Gage in his struggle for Section 30. It was a given fact the two men were at odds and each sought retribution. The continuing battle between the two strong-willed men became more than a local issue.

This curious case and bizarre proceedings sold extra copies of newspapers throughout California and local headlines announced, "Matthew Gage is hot after Judge Houghton" and "Spicy Suit Filed."[2] It promised to be a celebrated case with a prominent citizen attempting to disbar a popular California barrister. As the case unfolded, the *Riverside Daily Press* reported to their readers; "The Press will not take a stand in the Gage-Houghton controversy believing such matters at issue are for the courts rather than the newspapers to settle."[3]

Judge Joseph. S. Noyes had a full calendar of commitments and selected Judge Hughes of San Diego to hear the case. He knew Judge Hughes to be fair, competent and impartial. Mr. Houghton, however, objected to Judge Noyes' selection. Matthew, and his attorney, had no objection to Judge Hughes hearing the case.

At the time, Judge Noyes was a candidate seeking appointment for a superior court judgeship. His opponent was John G. North and their campaigns became exceedingly bitter. John North was defeated and never again took an active part in politics. Rumors circulated that North's vindictive attitude towards Noyes was a result of his lenient rulings in Matthew Gage's cases.

Witness Perry Corl, a Riverside photographer, testified that Mr. Houghton came to his gallery with Newman, Gunther and Atwater while he was developing photographs requested by Mr. Houghton. The photos were to be presented to the Department of the Interior in Washington D.C. Corl had taken pictures of Atwater's house and grounds, as well as other views of Section 30. The entry men and their attorney examined the negatives and, the following day, Corl delivered the prints to Mr. Houghton at the Glenwood Hotel, where he was staying. The photographer did not know who had added the incorrect inscriptions identifying Atwater's house. Gage was emphatic that the photograph had no relationship to the place it claimed to represent. The house was that of Otto Lowentrout's, located on Section 25, not Section 30. Witnesses testified that they thought the inscription attached to the photograph in question read, "View from" residence of W. E. Atwater instead of "residence of" Atwater.

Mr. Atwater testified that he had not seen the finished photographs until they appeared in court. He could not explain the error of his initials, W. A. Atwater, instead of W. E., that appeared beneath the photo representing his house and stated that he wouldn't have made such an error on his initials. Newman testified that Mr. Houghton did not know of the error until the suit was tried before the Secretary of the Interior when he read the inscription on Exhibit Number 57 and found it incorrect. Gunther reported that until the suit, Mr. Houghton did not know picture 57 was improperly labeled.[4]

When Matthew Gage testified, he stated that he had been in Washington from January 1895 until April 1896. Mr. Houghton asked what he was doing there and Gage answered, "watching Mr. Houghton." He further stated that he had not seen the mislabeled photos at the hearing before the Secretary of the Interior. Later, he examined government files and records and, after considerable effort, discovered the pictures had been improperly filed.

After a month of court proceedings, Judge Hughes' decision was brief and comprehensive - "no appeal." Judge R. E. Houghton of San Francisco was not disbarred from the practice of law in California. County Clerk Mr. W. W. Phelps received the following decision on Saturday, March 31, 1900:

> "Dear Sir:-In the matter of the application for the disbarment of R. E. Houghton Judgment will be rendered for the defendant.
>
> Respectively, J. W. Hughes."

The case was one of the most notable and spirited legal fights ever witnessed in Riverside. The entire question hinged on the photographs used in the famous fight over possession of Section 30. Allegations implied Mr. Houghton knew the inscriptions on Exhibit 57 were false when he introduced them

Riverside's Street Fair on Main Street 1900

before the Secretary of the Interior. *The Press & Horticulturist* reported, "Judge Hughes evidently believed that Houghton was blameless in the matter, and so ruled in his favor."[5] The judgment, however, did not completely vindicate him in the eyes of the general public and Matthew continued to consider him a deceitful foe.

During the course of the disbarment suit, citizens in Riverside were planning a professionally organized street fair celebrating the importance and value of its citrus industry. The Twenty-Eighth Agricultural District Fair sponsored the eight-day event held during the middle of April 1900. The Glenwood Hotel was still recovering from a destructive January fire that had damaged the north wing, limiting available rooms. A kettle of grease on the stove had boiled over and caught fire and spread rapidly through one wing. Hotel guests evacuated the premises after the 11:15 p.m. blaze and fortunately all were safe and given new rooms.[6]

It took months before Frank Miller collected insurance claims. Painters and carpenters then remained busy in April repairing fire damage. The general purpose of the festival was to publicize Riverside's excellent climate, exceptional water systems, and the prominence of the navel orange.

Main Street, from Seventh to Ninth, was lined with 64 booths, each brightly decorated with signs representing sponsoring organizations. Huge tents attracted visitors who enjoyed a variety of exhibits and demonstrations. One contained four stages where band concerts and speeches took place while another housed a detailed display of local water supplies. Individual water companies issued brochures listing their services and colored maps of the route of the world famous Gage Canal. Matthew Gage and family attended the spectacular street fair where the hero of the day was Luther Tibbets. The 79-year-old received accolades for his part in introducing the world-famous navel orange to Riverside.[7]

Luther occupied a special booth, sponsored by a local businessman, where he held court each day. Here, he had the opportunity to visit old acquaintances and recount his personal memories connected with the introduction of the original navel orange trees. He recalled moving from Washington D. C. in 1872 and settling on government land in Riverside with his wife, Eliza. She later wrote a friend, William Saunders, superintendent of the Botanical Gardens in the Department of Agriculture, seeking trees of the navel orange variety imported from Brazil.[8]

Tibbets smiled as he remembered the two small trees received through the mail packed in moss with bare roots. It was a miracle that they survived the month-long trip and the winter transplanting. This was Luther's last public appearance. After years of litigation over land titles and water rights, Luther Tibbets died in July 1902, penniless and with few friends. At the conclusion of the highly successful 1900 street fair, Riverside newspapers proudly reported, "Not one bottle of wine was exhibited at the fair."

Priestley Hall's mule streetcar service had been absorbed by the *Riverside & Arlington Railroad* in 1895 for the sum of one dollar and cancellation of a $490 debt. Priestley Hall and his family received lifelong passes over all R & A streetcar lines. Old rails were removed and a new electrified system operated from downtown to the north end of the Victoria Bridge. The slightly altered streetcar route continued to accommodate the Gage family on Fourteenth Street.

James Roe passed away in the summer of 1900 in Los Angeles. His many friends attended services held in his Riverside home on Lemon Street and paid their respects to an honorable man. He was remembered as first editor of the *Riverside Press* and for his compiled remembrances of early Riverside known as Roe's Notes. With Roe's death, Matthew lost another close friend, one of his earliest supporters and critics. His small jewelry shop in Roe's Drug Store represented a happy time in his life, mainly due to James Roe's jovial disposition and his interesting collection of customers.

In the early 1900s a major water issue surfaced when the Riverside Trust Company tried to assess the East Riverside Water Company for improvements to the Gage Canal.[9] The charge was for new pumping plants and renovations to the canal south of the Tequesquite Arroyo. Matthew Gage's original deed of November 10, 1886 to the Iowa Land & Development Company, and to its successor East Riverside Water Company, "conveyed delivery of water with the expense of pumping not included in the cost of maintaining and repairing." Gage did not extend his canal to Arlington Heights until 1888, two years after committing water to the Iowa Syndicate.

Directors of the East Riverside Water Company filed a cross-complaint stating that Matthew Gage's agreement and deed read:

"From the time of delivery it shall bear its proportionate share of running expenses of canal but not for enlarging or cementing thereof."

Victoria Avenue 1900

Finally, on October 14, 1909, the United States Circuit Court of Appeal upheld Matthew Gage's deed of November 10, 1886, declaring that the East Riverside Water Company had no interest in the canal beyond its point of delivered water. This important case upheld the legality of Matthew Gage's recorded deeds and agreements that were automatically transferred to his successor, the Riverside Trust Company.

Matthew was involved in building a third floor onto his house in October 1900. At the time, Charles E. Maud, manager of the Trust Company packinghouse, was in London conferring with top officials. Two weeks after he returned, Mr. Crewdson and Mr. Dickinson, directors of the Riverside Trust Company, arrived in Riverside and registered at the Glenwood Hotel. Painters and carpenters had completed repairs to the building damaged in a January fire and new furnishings and an enlarged dining room had been added.

The Englishmen had come to inspect the property and operations of the Trust company. They observed the growth of their citrus groves, investigated conditions at the ranch houses, and scrutinized operations of the packinghouse. After several days of appraisals, they decided to make substantial changes in the interests of the company. In the meantime, a strong storm with heavy rain interfered with their daily assessments and the gentlemen were obliged to extend their stay through Thanksgiving. Frank and Isabella Miller entertained the distinguished guests with a traditional American turkey dinner, served with all the trimmings.

Mr. Crewdson and Mr. Dickinson initiated critical changes in management of the Trust Company's interests. William Irving, heretofore manager of the entire Trust Company properties, became consulting manager and engineer of the company. William Fraser, former bookkeeper, became manager and John M. Mylne became William Irving's assistant engineer. A major reorganization entailed all planted lands and ranch houses and the Riverside Orange Company would be administered by the Arlington Heights Fruit Company.[10] With the union of these companies, the Arlington Heights Fruit Company became one of the largest citrus fruit shippers in Riverside. The visiting Englishmen made one other significant change before returning to England. They ordered   the new Arlington Heights Fruit Company to join the Riverside Fruit Exchange, a cooperative marketing firm. The decision to become a member of the exchange, and share its fortunes, "was entirely unsolicited" reported the *Press Enterprise*.[11]

This organizational shake-up left citizens wondering why such drastic steps had been taken and if such substantial changes were truly necessary. William Fraser, a bookkeeper, knew little about agricultural management and, consequently, reliable employees such as Charles Maud's brother, and others, found work elsewhere. Increasingly, Matthew Gage felt that he must gain control of the Trust Company.

In order to continue developing Arlington Heights, large work crews became a necessity and three major labor camps were built at convenient locations. These compounds known as Windsor, Balmoral and Osborne, were named for the homes of English royalty.[12] These living quarters incorporated bunkhouses, kitchens, dining rooms, stables and equipment storage sheds.

On Christmas Day, Matthew Gage had a pleasant surprise when a newspaper article praised his Section 30.

> Near Eighth Street is the nicest orange grove in the valley. Level as a plain, the richest soil in the valley and as good a water right as exists, all these advantages this tract possesses. A year ago Section 30 was as barren as the desert. The tract is the famous Section 30 which has been in litigation for two decades.

> Now the portion along Eighth Street is as pretty as a young grove anywhere in the valley. By the decision of the court a year ago last summer, the section was awarded Matthew Gage and by a subsequent withdrawal of claims, title is absolutely clear. Land has been graded and planted and in a few years this much litigated desert tract will become the most valuable orchard property in the valley.[13]

With the advent of a new year, 1901, Matthew was again in need of money, so Jane sold 40 acres of Block 65 in Arlington Heights for $33,000. Cornelius Rumsey, treasurer of the American Cracker Company, purchased the property and moved to Riverside to improve his failing health. Later that year, he built an 11-room house on Victoria Avenue, adjacent to his citrus grove.[14] The impressive frame house became a local landmark and Cornelius Rumsey was recognized as a prominent businessman, highly respected in the community.

Matthew, once again, escorted his ladies to a happy family wedding in January when Margaret Eva Irving married

Cornelius Rumsey House, Victoria Avenue, 1903

Canadian Ernest Stewart Malloch in Calvary Presbyterian Church at high noon. With the strains of the matchless wedding march, William Irving proudly walked down the isle with his beautiful daughter. The six brides-maids, including Maude Gage, were gowned in cream satin with tiny velvet boleros. The dresses had high neck lines and the young girls wore long elbow length gloves.

At the conclusion of the church ceremony, friends and relatives were welcomed at Raeburn, where a festive reception took place. The bride's gifts to her attendants were golden bowknots, trimmed in pearls, and the groom presented ties to his ushers, one of whom was handsome Henry Henderson.[15] Matthew and Jane enjoyed the family celebration and visiting with their many nieces and nephews. A group of young people followed the newlyweds to the train station where they left for San Francisco, the first stop before a five month honeymoon in Europe.

In less than a week, this happy occasion was sadly followed by the death of beloved Queen Victoria. Combined church services were held in Calvary Presbyterian Church where a large portrait of the Queen had been draped in British and American flags and altar railings held draped black crepe. Pastors of various dominations filled the chairs of honor in front of the church and each had a comment about the departed Queen. One minister said it all: "As a woman, as a Christian, as a wife, as a mother, as the Queen of a great empire, she has been deserving of all honor."[16] Another speaker dazzled the audience with extraordinary figures and predictions:

> Queen Victoria had 83 children, grandchildren, and great grandchildren, of whom 71 are living and 12 are dead. She has not only been a great Queen, but a mother of kings, queens, and emperors. No other royal family has ever held within the circle of its membership so many crowns and scepters. The descendants of Queen Victoria have already assured to them the thrones of the two great empires, Great Britain and Germany and within 20 years, that of Britain, Germany, and Russia will all be worn at the same time by her children.[17]

The foundation of the Robert Henderson's house, Edgemont, was left untouched, in order to firm and compact during the winter of 1900. Mr. Henderson's business commitments had also delayed construction. The original plans, drawn by a New York architect, had to be revised by Robert Gage to conform to the hilltop building site. A reservoir was built and a street was graded above Victoria Avenue for access to the Henderson house and the nearby John Mylne house named Greystones. The short dirt road,

Edgemont, The Robert Henderson House, Hawarden Drive

called Hawarden Drive, connected the Henderson, Mylne and Irving houses.

When construction resumed the following spring, carpenters requested an eight-hour day to replace their previous 10-hour day. They also asked for the same wage of $3 a day.[18] Four years after acquiring the property, the Robert Hendersons moved into their elegantly furnished hilltop house. Mr. Henderson incorporated the Riverside Fruit Company, a local fruit packing and shipping company.

In April, Mrs. Robert Henderson, Jennet, held a grand reception celebrating the completion of their castle-like house named Edgemont. More than two hundred prestigious matrons and young ladies were invited to the afternoon social event of the year.

Jane Gage and her attractive daughters attended the fashionable reception at Edgemont, where Margaret had the honor of presenting white carnations to arriving guests. Maude assisted her Aunt Eliza, Mrs. William Irving, who presided over the coffee urn.[19] The Henderson house, with its grand staircase, colorful stained-glass windows and park-like grounds, earned many compliments from the invited guests who would always remember the delightful afternoon party.

Matthew continued traveling to England where he served as a director of the board of the Trust Company. During his absence, Jane and their daughters were invited to many social affairs and the Gages remained part of Riverside's social scene. Margaret, 32, Maude, 26, Anna, 16, and Katherine, 13 were included in a variety of cultural activities, most often church affairs. Jane Gage's name appeared in the local newspaper column, "The Social Circles," after attending ladies' luncheons and whist parties. The card game of whist entailed no bidding and later evolved into a form of party bridge. Hostesses presented prizes to ladies accumulating the highest points and these afternoon affairs became delightful diversions for the Gage ladies. Irving and Gage family gatherings were frequent as they celebrated birthdays, holidays and special occasions.

Section 30 controversy sprang to life once again when the most incredible legal proceedings occurred in the spring of 1902. Gunther and Newman appealed Riverside Superior Court Judge Noyes' 1899 decision granting the square mile property to Matthew Gage. Citizens had assumed this to be a closed case. William Atwater had tired of the struggle and removed his house and outbuildings and relinquished all claims to the property. Gunther and Newman, however, still questioned the validity of Gage's claim, regardless of three previous cases before Judge Noyes who had rendered judgment in favor of Gage. The Supreme Court of California upheld the judgment of the lower court making a final decision in favor of Matthew Gage. *The Riverside Daily Press* reported:

> This will give title to Mr. Gage to property worth half a million dollars. It will probably end the long-drawn out controversy.

With the litigation resolved and a clear title, Matthew sold 190 acres of Section 30 and 40 inches of Gage Canal water to J. A. Bohon for $50,000.[20]

In the fall of 1902, Hugh G. Newton of London, England, purchased 52 acres of land south of Victoria Avenue near Madison Street in Arlington Heights. For the sum of $20,000, the young Englishman received a deed from Milton J. Daniels, president of Orange Growers Bank as trustee. On the same day, Newton bought 15 acres from the Riverside Trust Company for $20. The price discrepancy may have been due to the fact that his father, Thomas Henry Goodwin Newton, Esquire, of Barrels, Henley-in-Arden, England, was chairman of the Riverside Trust Company and the majority stockholder.[21]

Young Newton and his charming wife, Adelaide, moved to Riverside and had a one-story marble block house built upon their hilltop property overlooking their orange grove. Many people believed Hugh to be a remittance man from a privileged English family, living with a trust fund and no need to work. Others wondered if he was sent to observe the Trust Company operations and Frasier's management skills. Whatever their ultimate purpose, however, Riverside welcomed the young couple and their novel English customs.

Adelaide, friendly and attractive, possessed few domestic skills, but somehow managed to prepare nightly meals. The young couple routinely dined in formal attire.[22] Hugh left the cultivation and management of his orange groves in the hands of the Arlington Heights Fruit Company, providers of complete grove care. The company advertised "personal attention to grove care, picking and marketing and satisfaction to investors and resident growers."[23]

Hugh befriended 36-year-old Frank Tetley, an aspiring entrepreneur dealing in real estate. Tetley had moved to Riverside in 1886, became Frank Miller's secretary and bookkeeper and, from Miller, became interested in real estate. Riverside County government offices moved into the new county courthouse in 1904 leaving the Arlington Hotel empty and needing repair. In January 1906, Frank Tetley and Hugh Newton would purchase the three-story building for $30,000 and change its name to The Tetley Hotel.

In December 1903, Matthew was in London to secure cooperation of other shareholders in obtaining necessary shares to take over control of the Trust Company. Mr. T. H. G. Newton, chairman of the company and largest shareholder, became a sympathetic ally and offered to loan Matthew money to secure additional shares. Matthew refused to put any more money into the company unless he was given absolute control of its Riverside affairs.

Mr. Newton, a displeased shareholder, apparently agreed to Matthew Gage's takeover plans. The two men proposed uniting their shares, thus giving them enough voting power to remove five current directors and appoint four new members who shared their points of view. The Newton-Gage plan would place Newton in charge as chairman of the new board and Matthew would become managing director for all the company's California properties. On December 16, 1903, T. H. G. Newton loaned Matthew $145,000, all due and payable on June 16, 1904 plus interest of 10 percent. As security for the loan, Newton held a mortgage on 60 acres in Arlington Heights and Gage's personal property, My Sweet Anna.

One month later, in January 1904, Matthew Gage wrote to Mr. Newton in London:

> The best possibility for the accomplishment of this end by you is to have your son Mr. Hugh Newton appointed to my place on the board thereby restoring the agreed proposition upon which the new board was constituted, namely for two seats. You should surely be able to trust your own flesh and blood, in order to enable you to carry out the solemn covenant between us and I am abundantly satisfied Mr. Hugh would well and truly perform all the duties and functions in the premises.[24]

Mr. Newton apparently began to question Matthew's accusations of the Trust Company's dishonorable transactions. The following month, on February 23, 1904, Mr. and Mrs. Thomas Goodwin Newton registered at the new Glenwood Mission Inn for a pleasant visit with their son and daughter-in-law. While in Riverside, Mr. Newton quietly investigated rumors of wrongdoings sanctioned by the Riverside Trust Company that had been reported from various sources. Whatever transpired from his fact-finding inquires was never revealed. Mr. and Mrs. Newton suddenly left Riverside and, the following day, Hugh and Adelaide returned to England permanently as well.

Neighbors were surprised at their sudden departure without notice and rumors circulated that the young couple had been bestowed titles, Lord and Lady Newton, and were forced to leave immediately.[25] Other stories had to do with the couple inheriting a fortune. No one really knew why they left town in such a hurry but when the patriarch of the family ordered them back to England, they left immediately.

CHAPTER 11

In February and March, 1904, great excitement erupted throughout the Gage household in preparation for an upcoming wedding, the first in the Matthew Gage family. Jose cleaned and groomed the grounds and Maria assisted Jane and the girls in cleaning and sprucing up the house

On March 8, a license to wed was issued to Henry Banks Henderson, age 31, native of New York, and Maude Louise Gage, age 27, native of Canada. The popular couple, active members of the social Casa Blanca Tennis Club and of the new Victoria Club, had made many friends. Henry was employed as secretary-treasurer of his father's Riverside Fruit Company, packers and shippers of citrus fruit.[1] Maude

Matthew Gage's House 1900s

and Jean, Henry's sister, were good friends and Maude often visited the Henderson's hilltop home above Victoria Avenue.

The simple morning wedding took place in the north wing of the Gage's drawing room, artistically silhouetted with small palms, ferns and garlands of flowers draped over door frames. Only family members were present for the quiet, subdued ceremony. Maude exemplified the perfect bride in her embroidered chiffon dress, trimmed in tiny pearls and intricate lace. Her wedding veil of tulle complemented her bouquet of lilies of the valley. She was assisted by her 18-year-old sister, Anna, and Henry's groomsman was his brother William.[2]

After the modest religious ceremony for family members, guests were invited to the wedding reception. Matthew and Jane wished Maude and Henry a blissful, happy life together. Unfortunately, in the years ahead the marriage proved to be not so blissful.

It was a hot summer day on September 7, registering 110 degrees, the hottest day in 1904. William Irving had not been feeling well for several weeks and the hot weather did not add to his comfort. Two weeks later, the 71-year-old gentleman passed away in Raeburn, his stately eight-year-old home.[3] His sons, William Gage, Robert, and Norman, and his daughter, Kathleen, were great comfort to their mother, Eliza. According to William Irving's wishes, his simple service took place in his home with little fanfare and no music. Several tributes from friends noted his many contributions to the community and his "strong convictions about right and wrong." William Irving was buried in the Gage plot in Olivewood Cemetery. Matthew had previously paid $700 to increase the size of the family plot in Olivewood to accommodate all family members.[4]

A month after William Irving's death, his eldest daughter, Elizabeth, gave birth to twin girls, Enid and Kathleen. They were a great joy to Eliza Irving who continued to live out her life at Raeburn, with her six children and many grandchildren living nearby. However, she lost the good

Gage Canal delivering water

companionship of her brother, Robert Gage, and his wife, Mary, when they moved to Utica, New York, to be near their daughter, Janie. In June 1898, she had married Dr. T. H. Farrell of Utica whose medical practice was in Utica.[5] With William Fraser as general manager of the Trust Company's Riverside enterprises, and the death of his brother-in-law, William Irving, 63-year-old Robert Gage perhaps wanted a change. Matthew truly missed his brother's counsel, his stability and his devotion. Robert's affiliation with the Westminster Presbyterian Church of Utica began October 27, 1904, and ended with his death in 1925.

By 1904, Matthew Gage was in financial trouble again. When Mr. T. H. G. Newton's six-month loan became due on June 16, 1904, Matthew had not paid one cent towards either principal or interest. The following year, John G. North, Newton's Riverside attorney, filed a suit in the United States Circuit Court to foreclose on Gage's property to recover $146,100, plus accrued interest.[6] The mortgage encumbered 60 acres in Block 65 of Arlington Heights. Examination of County Recorder records disclosed that Matthew Gage had other outstanding mortgages, notably to G. Howard Thompson of the Bank of California and to First National Bank of Riverside. Thus began a new tangle of injunctions, foreclosures, law suits, and animosities.

During the winter of 1904-1905, local citrus growers commissioned Charles Hatfield to produce rain. He was known as The Rainmaker and gained a reputation as a "wizard" by producing much-needed rain for southern California farmers.

Maude Henderson
with son Gage

He used a mysterious apparatus installed on a tall tower to gain altitude for his chemical mixtures. Riverside's annual rainfall for 1904-1905 totaled 16.78 inches. Charlie Hatfield took all the credit, collected his fee, and became even more popular as a weather magician.[7]

Despite continued wet weather, June remained a popular month for weddings. Chauncey McFarland, the mayor of Riverside, married Jean Henderson on June 2 at her parent's home, Edgemont. Her good friend, and sister-in-law, Maude Gage Henderson, did not participate in the wedding as she was five months pregnant. On November 29, 1905, Henry and Maude became proud parents of a son named Gage Henderson, commemorating the Gage family name. Jane and Matthew became doting grandparents and Margaret, Anna and Katherine were attentive aunties. Matthew's life was enlivened with the addition to the family.

The day after Gage Henderson's birth, a group of enthusiastic car drivers held its first annual hill climbing contest by racing up Box Springs Grade. Matthew's Section 30 received much scrutiny and attention, as the races starting point was on Eighth Street bordering his property. A steady parade of cars, carriages, bicycles and pedestrians filed down Eighth Street to watch powerful cars climb the steep hill. An assortment of autos rambled into town and parked near Section 30 to watch Ramblers, Maxwells, Reliances and other cars start up the hill. Every five minutes a car left the starting point and was carefully timed until it crossed the finish line. The first prize went to a Reliance and a Rambler won second place.[8]

In December, Wilson Crewdson registered at the Glenwood Mission Inn for his annual inspection trip of Arlington Heights. He had first visited the Glenwood Hotel in 1884, where he spent part of his honeymoon. He looked forward to renewing his friendship with Frank Miller and it had become his custom to present his host a remembrance gift upon departing. In 1905, he gave Frank Miller an unusual silver English post horn, five feet in length, for gathering crowds and gaining attention.[9] The previous year he had given his host a 1775 print of William Penn signing a treaty with the Indians. Crewdson's 1905 visit was brief and it is doubtful that Frank Miller mentioned the Englishman's visit to his friend, Matthew Gage.

On occasion, Riverside newspaper articles touted the continuing prosperity and progress taking place in Arlington Heights. Whenever Matthew read these glowing attributes, he could not help thinking about what could have been his personal property. In 1905, the *Riverside Daily Press* reported:

Arlington Heights Fruit Company, the Riverside Orange Company, and the Riverside Trust Company all are companies representing large investments of

English capital. The Riverside Trust Company owns all of Arlington Heights which it developed at great cost, grading streets and avenues and planting shade and ornamental trees. The entire tract is subdivided into five and 10 acre lots and planted to Washington navels and valencias. Much land has been sold to individual orange growers but the company still holds some 1500-acres of groves. The Riverside Orange Company is owner of 600-acres of oranges and lemons which it holds as an investment. Arlington Heights Fruit Company is an auxiliary company organized for the purpose of packing and marketing fruit grown by the Trust Company, Riverside Orange Company, and other growers in Arlington Heights who market their fruit through the California Fruit Growers Exchange. W. G. Fraser is general manager of all the companies, James Mills is superintendent of the Land Department, and Fred Little is in charge of packinghouse operations.[10]

On December 6, 1905, Jane Gage became involved in Matthew's legal affairs when she filed action to enjoin foreclosure suits amounting to $300,000, alleging that she executed mortgages on the explicit promise of Mr. Newton to help her husband gain control of the Riverside Trust Company. She claimed that her husband carried out his part of their agreement, but Mr. Newton had resigned from the board and left the company's management in the hands of those hostile to her husband.

On December 22, 1905, Matthew filed a suit, through his attorneys, Purington & Adair, in the Federal Court in Los Angeles asking for the court to appoint a receiver to take charge of the assets of the Riverside Trust Company, Limited. Voluminous documents, numbering 300 pages, detailed transactions from the company's inception to the present time and were included in the filings. Matthew's accusations were considered sensational and newspapers throughout the state followed the suit carefully.

His complaint alleged that he had received only $150,000 and was due at least an additional $750,000. He claimed to have spent half a million dollars on completion of the extended irrigation system for which he was never compensated. Furthermore, he said, the Trust Company's new directors had forced him out of the company by means of undisclosed documents and contracts. He acknowledged having spent large sums of borrowed money to cultivate and develop Arlington Heights before the Trust Company took over the land and water system. According to his petition, he had spent $350,000 in improvements and during a five-year period the property value had increased to an estimated $5,000,000.[11] According to his figures, the improved property should return a net annual income of $250,000.

Matthew Gage said he had an agreement with T. H. G. Newton to borrow $300,000 to secure enough shares to control the company. He had delivered his Trust Company shares to Mr. Newton in London as part of the security for the loan. After gaining control, he anticipated completing various projects that he had long advocated. When opposing board members became aware of his plan, Matthew claimed that the directors promptly executed a deed of trust to three

Victoria Avenue

Englishmen, namely Wilson Crewdson and two London lawyers retained by the Trust Company. This involved 60 acres in Block 65 in Arlington Heights that Jane Gage had mortgaged to Mr. Newton.

Matthew asked the court to appoint a receiver to take charge of the property until such time it could be sold.[12] Matthew predicted that his share, after disposal of the holdings, would total approximately $2,500,000.

Readers of the local *Press & Horticulturalist* found an article announcing that Robert Bettner had sold the Hugh Newton property in Arlington Heights to two local businessmen for $45,000. The Newton property consisted of 52 acres of oranges and 24 acres vacant, plus a marble block bungalow built by T. H. G. Newton's son, Hugh, and his wife Adelaide.[13]

Judge Ross of the United States Federal Court of Los Angeles, in the action of Newton versus Gage, ruled foreclosure proceedings against Matthew Gage and refused his request to appoint a receiver for the Riverside Trust Company. Furthermore, the Judge issued a restraining order restricting Jane Gage from interfering with Newton's rights to the mortgaged property, mainly removal of 1,400 boxes of oranges grown on the property. Mr. Newton had paid all expenses on the property, including taxes, since the note was instigated in December 1904.

Matthew, not satisfied with the outcome, began another suit against the Trust Company in February 1906. His attorney J. S. Chapman filed a suit asking for damages in the amount of $2,500,000.[14] The estimate of damages was based upon the value of Matthew's 1400 A-shares of stock and 900 B-shares and upon the anticipated income generated if the company had been administered according to his ideas. This case complemented his earlier one in 1899, charging the Riverside Trust Company with manipulating records in order to diminish dividend payments. Matthew's case was delayed for months and the general public was losing interest in his continual legal entanglements.

Bold headlines spread across the front page of the *Riverside Daily Press* announced, "Earth's Awful Tremor at 5:15 a.m. in San Francisco - Brought Death and Disaster." As Matthew read the April 18, 1906 evening edition, he prayed for the safety of his friends and business associates in the demolished city. Riverside had not experienced any movement from the gigantic quake or aftershocks that had devastated San Francisco and surrounding cities. One sharp shock did most of the damage, breaking water mains and demolishing stately buildings. Flames could not be extinguished in the bay area as smoke from more than 50 fires blocked out the sun, turning the sky bright red.

Santa Rosa and Oakland were severely damaged and residents huddled together in parks and open places, reluctant to venture near buildings. Another strong shock hit at 11:24, destroying the Palace Hotel, City Hall, and the grand Opera House.[15] The Governor of California, George C. Pardee, sent telegrams to major cities, including Riverside, asking for immediate help. Riverside's Chamber of Commerce and most churches offered assistance in the emergency. Jane Gage and her daughters joined volunteers at Calvary Presbyterian Church, where men and women packed boxes of donated items for earthquake victims.

Local stores emptied their shelves of canned food, blankets, clothes and bedding and packed them for a speedy northern delivery. The Red Cross Society helped organize a Relief Fund and railroads shipped all goods free to San Francisco. Reports from damaged areas were staggering.

Forty-five men of Company M, a local National Guard Unit, dressed in khaki uniforms with full equipment, were sent north to distribute and guard provisions from looters. One month after the quake, requests were still coming to Riverside for donations of clothes and church ladies continued peddling sewing machines, putting together shirts, skirts, and pants.[16] After the quake, when currency became scarce, the San Francisco Mint released uncirculated silver dollars, dating back to 1879.

Before the 1906 San Francisco earthquake, Henry E. Huntington, president of the Pacific Electric Company, had acquired the financially troubled *Riverside & Arlington Railroad*. In 1903, he had appeared before the City Trustees with a proposal to build a scenic trolley line from downtown Riverside, across the Victoria Bridge, and along the median strip of Victoria Avenue.[17] At its terminus, the trolley line would then turn at Adams Street and join the Magnolia Avenue line. Townspeople agreed that the roadway would be a great tourist attraction and Henry Huntington was granted a franchise. For unknown reasons, Mr. Huntington failed to construct the proposed line within the three-year period set by the Trustees and the franchise expired in 1906. The Victoria Avenue trolley continued to run on the south side of the bridge where it stopped near the entrance to the Victoria Club.

Matthew's 1906 case against the Riverside Trust Company continued to be postponed, month after month. During this period, Judge Joseph S. Noyes was appointed to preside in the District Court of Appeal of the Second Appellate District, the first time such an honor had been bestowed upon a California Superior Court Judge.[18] Judge Noyes continued to serve the citizens of Riverside for seven more years until he retired and moved to Los Angeles to be near his grown children.

With the end of the navel orange season, transient farm workers moved on to work in the fields of Arizona. In late fall, Chinese laborers filtered into Chinatown seeking work in vineyards that were steadily disappearing. Citrus-related jobs increased with greater production at the same time that Japanese laborers arrived in Riverside. A sizeable Japanese village emerged near the Arlington Heights Fruit Company packinghouse on Madison Street. One large building housed over 50 workers and smaller Japanese communes were located around town.[19]

In November 1906, the Japanese community held a celebration in the Loring Opera House to honor the 57th birthday of Emperor Matsu Hito. Hundreds of people, of all

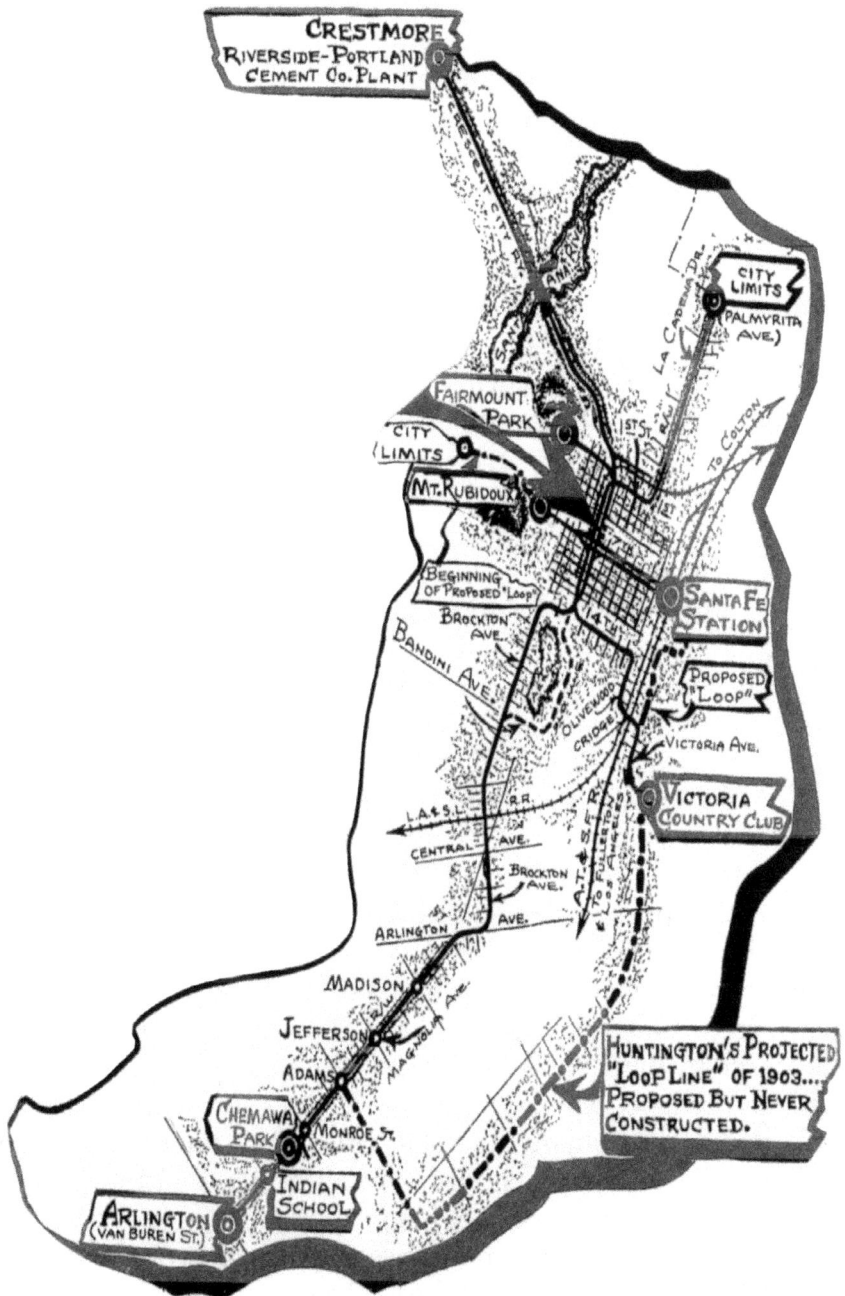

Proposed Victoria Avenue Streetcar Route

races, attended the happy gathering in the brightly decorated Opera House, where flags, lanterns and parasols greeted the audience. Vases of chrysanthemums, Japan's national flower, were proudly displayed throughout the building, adding color and brilliance. There were many speeches, in both Japanese and English, and Mayor Chauncey McFarland spoke highly of the Japanese people "as workers, as friends, and as neighbors." At the end of the evening ceremony everyone shouted "Banzi - Banzi, long live the Emperor."[20]

The year 1907 proved to be another troublesome time for Matthew and Jane. In March the *Riverside Daily Press* printed a notice of Sale under a Mortgage.

> Whereas Matthew and Jane Gage executed to G. Howard Thompson, a trustee of Bank of California, a mortgage dated July 15, 1903 and recorded in the office of the County Recorder of Riverside County, mortgaging property to secure the payment of a promissory note for the sum of $160,000 payable on or before January 1, 1904 with interest at six percent. Said mortgage will sell for cash by public auction on the 26th day of March, 1907, at the front door of the courthouse at twelve noon to the highest bidder.[21]

The property included 49 acres of producing orange trees in Section 30 and the Gage home place of ten acres on Fourteenth Street. The notice of sale also included 98 shares of Gage Canal stock. Mr. T. H. G. Newton's note had been acquired by Bank of California, represented by Mr. Thompson. Judge Bledsoe of the Superior Court of San Bernardino allowed a postponement of sale, due to arguments on points of law. Newspaper headlines announced, "Matthew Gage loses fight to prevent sale of his property."

On April 12, the foreclosure sale of Gage's property took place at noon on the steps of the Riverside County Courthouse. Before bidding commenced, Jane Gage announced that she had prior claims to the properties in question and any sale would be subject to results of previous litigation. Friends and adversaries of Matthew Gage were puzzled that he had not sold some land in Section 30 to recover his home place. His business dealings were becoming even more mystifying and unconventional.

The lone bidder was Frank A. Tetley, who stated that he made the offer on behalf of the San Francisco and Fresno Land Company. His bid of $15,000 on the home place and $45,000 for the remaining property was accepted.[22] Matthew Gage immediately filed a cross-complaint, demanding that the case be scheduled for oral arguments. Unfortunately, Judge Chapman died suddenly, postponing any action for nearly a year.

During the spring and summer of 1907, Americans were experiencing a general wave of prosperity and were spending money rather than saving. Bank deposits declined and financial organizations were overextended. A depressed stock market then created a run on most banks. Bank currency was limited and merchants and businesses were forced to accept certificates, cashier's checks, or scrip. In November 1907, the associated banks of Riverside issued paper scrip, in different colors denoting one, five, ten and twenty dollars, as a temporary currency to conduct business.[23] In December, Hugh Newton's former house in Arlington Heights was purchased by Doctor W. F. Fundenburg of Pittsburg, Pennsylvania for $57,000 cash. This cash sale helped to alleviate some problems experienced by local banks.

Matthew Gage's suit against the Riverside Trust Company finally came to a head in April 1909. Judge Bledsoe delivered his decision in favor of G. Howard Thompson, representing the Trust Company, stating that Matthew Gage was negligent in payment of over $50,000 due on the balance of a promissory note. The Judge reviewed Gage's difficulties and attempts to reorganize the Trust Company, including his failure to consummate a coup. Matthew Gage needed money to acquire as much stock as possible and had secured

Riverside County Courthouse 1903

a mortgage of $160,000 on his Riverside properties, and had surrendered his stock in the Trust Company as collateral.

Matthew claimed that Thompson, representing the bank and others, had played into the hands of his enemies, selling them the stock that he had pledged as security for the loan. His pledged stock, owned by his adversaries, was then used to vote against him. Gage also claimed the stock to be worth $780,000 but was sold to John G. North, acting for the opposing factions among the directorate, for only $83,500. Matthew Gage asked for damages totaling $1,500,000.[24]

Judge Bledsoe continued his reviews, stating that Matthew Gage had failed to pay any principal or interest on the promissory note. The stock had transferred from Newton to Thompson, representing the bank, and the bank had sold the stock in July 1906. The value of Matthew's shares was said to be problematic and Judge Bledsoe declared, "John G. North, Wilson Crewdson, and other officers of the Riverside Trust Company acted in good faith. The sale of the property was proper and in accordance with the terms of the mortgage." Headlines in the *Riverside Daily Press* disclosed, "Defeated in Action Brought Against Bank of California and Land Company. Gage Will Appeal Case."[25]

Matthew and Jane were despondent over the prospects of losing their home. They turned to their church for spiritual guidance to help them through the unpredictable days ahead and the ensuing Easter holiday. Their friend Frank Miller, then president of the local Chamber of Commerce, organized a committee to plan a sunrise Easter service at the foot of the cross atop Mount Rubidoux on April 2, 1909. The Gage family, however, joined the Calvary Presbyterian Church congregation to welcome and support their new minister, Doctor W. A. Hunter from Denver, Colorado.

Later that year, in September, Frank Miller's daughter Allis married DeWitt Hutchings in a simple ceremony witnessed only by her father. Margaret and Maude remembered when they were little girls and how they had held baby Allis. The Gage family extended best wishes to the newlyweds.

Newspapers were full of President William Howard Taft's visit to Riverside on October 12, 1909, when Frank Miller escorted the honored guest to the peak of Mount Rubidoux to unveil a plaque honoring Father Junipero Serra, an early Franciscan monk.[26] The President was impressed with the beauty of citrus groves spread over hundreds of acres. President Taft's visit concluded with a gala reception at the Glenwood Mission Inn where he was seated in a specially made oversized chair.

Two days after President Taft's visit, the United States Court of Appeal upheld Matthew Gage's deeds and agreements with the East Riverside Land Company in dealing with Gage Canal assessments. He was beholden to the Chaffey brothers for their valuable advice concerning water rights, laws and the importance of recording all legal documents.

Riverside was a growing community in 1909. City officials were unable to estimate the demographic growth of the community and awaited results from the upcoming thirteenth census of the United States in 1910.

GAGE IRRIGATION CANAL (1885-1889)

Riverside Water Company and Gage Canal Systems

CHAPTER 12

The year 1910 began with heavy rains. The Santa Ana River filled with debris washed down from surrounding mountains. Gloomy weather added to the depressing news that John Greenleaf North had died on January 10 in London, England. He had left Riverside before Christmas to take depositions there concerning the Bank of California versus Matthew Gage case. Mr. North had influenza before leaving New York, but felt well enough to make the journey. When he arrived in England, however, he became gravely ill and required medical attention. Wilson Crewdson, of the Riverside Trust Company, sent cablegrams to William Frasier in Riverside informing him of John North's illness and later of his death.

Sorrow engulfed the town of Riverside. John Greenleaf North had been an early settler who assisted his father, John Wesley North, in establishing the Riverside colony. He had married, had four sons, and after resigning as manager-superintendent of the Riverside Water Company, had become a successful citrus grower and nurseryman. Tragically, he had experienced serious financial losses in 1893 when a severe frost destroyed $50,000 of nursery stock, leaving him penniless.[1] Undaunted, he took up the practice of law, passed the California bar at age 42 and became a prominent, respected attorney, one of the foremost in the state.

The *Riverside Daily Press* devoted a special column reviewing John G. North's life and describing his strong, unyielding personality.

> This Riversider had more than his share of enemies and his faults and his virtues were those of a strong, true, positive character. He learned to become a good lawyer, one firmly grounded in the principles of the law. He was absolutely uncompromising in respect to

his views of right and wrong, and did not know the meaning of quit.

John North, a widower, left an estate of $168,000 to his grown sons. City resolutions and organizational ceremonies commemorated the life of John G. North, a community leader who would be missed.

Four months later, on Sunday morning May 15, 1910, the town trembled with a strong earthquake that lasted several seconds. Bric-a-brac toppled off shelves, walls cracked and bricks fell from chimneys. Matthew and family had become seasoned to "temblors" and took the latest quake in stride.

Two days later, attorney William Gage Irving submitted dismissals to be entered in actions of Jane Gage versus Matthew Gage; San Francisco & Fresno Land Company versus Jane Gage and others, and G. Howard Thompson versus Matthew Gage.[2] The controversial, but sentimental, trial in Superior Court was expeditiously cancelled with all parties in agreement. This unpredicted vindication on the part of all parties meant "removal from the court's consideration and dismissal of all charges." It also was the conclusion of any litigation by Matthew Gage in his attempt to secure control of the Riverside Trust Company.

Whatever transpired between contesting parties remains unknown, but from these overlapping law suits and foreclosures, Matthew and Jane somehow managed to retain the use of their home place for life. Nevertheless, the Bank of California did take control of the adjacent Gage citrus grove and its management. Friends and associates often wondered if Matthew's encumbered property prevented him from selling off portions of Section 30 to save title to his home.

Pessimistic souls believed such an act of kindness by bank officials may have been due to the fact the end of the world was imminent. Halley's Comet was passing between the sun and earth and this unusual phenomenon produced real fear and alarm to many people. Some feared that the comet's tail contained deadly gas that would kill every

William Gage Irving

living thing and local physicians reported increasing numbers
of nervous breakdowns and extra nurses were hired at the
Brockton Avenue hospital. Sleeping potions became available
so one could remain asleep when the earth passed through
the comet's tail.[3]

Parents kept their children home from school and
families gathered together when the world was to end.
The phenomenon of Halley's Comet ended after the earth

successfully passed through its tail giving the sun a veiled reddish tinge.

In the spring of 1910, the Gage family acquired a new dog, Prince. He was confined to an area near the house behind a sturdy fence and spent his nights with Jose and Maria. Their precautions were brought about by an epidemic of rabies and carried by an abundance of stray dogs. City officials issued the following notice in local newspapers: "All dogs must be muzzled and if found running at large will be taken up and killed without further notice."[4] Matthew and Jane were thankful for their strong fence and flinched at the sound of gunshots.

Matthew's close confidante was his 40-year-old nephew, William Gage Irving, who was like a son to Jane and a brother to his daughters. In 1910, he was appointed City Attorney, a notable accomplishment for such a young man. Matthew and William spent many leisure hours discussing city matters and world affairs. William often spent the night at the Fourteenth Street house rather than travel several miles to Raeburn where he resided with his mother, Eliza Irving.

The men discussed Arlington Heights affairs and the proposed new improvements, especially the planting of palm trees along Victoria Avenue that spring. In December 1910, however, the gentlemen exchanged views on the widower Frank Miller's recent wedding to Marion Clark. Marion, a local resident, had been Miller's secretary for a number of years and had traveled east to attend a "finishing" school. The Millers were married in a simple ceremony in the Buckingham Hotel in New York and upon their return to Riverside, citizens welcomed them home. A certain amount of gossip resulted concerning their 27 year age difference. Frank and Marion Miller proved to be an ideal couple, devoted to one another.

In February 1911, Frank Miller, assisted by Matthew Gage and others, opened the Riverside International Peace Conference in the new wing of the Glenwood Mission Inn. Known as the Cloister Music Room, it extended along Orange

Street where advocates met to share their views on ways to stop wars and maintain world peace.

Andrew Carnegie, a man of wealth and influence, encouraged all such gatherings and contributed to the Riverside conference. Europe and Asia were on the brink of wars and a vigorous peace policy advanced across the nation. Church congregations heard sermons describing the perils of war and Dr. W. A. Hunter of the Calvary Presbyterian Church lectured on the hazards of combat.

All advocates of world peace were invited to the conference and an array of dignitaries gathered in the Music Room of the Mission Inn on February 27. John Muir, the naturalist; Charles W. Fairbanks, former Vice-President of the United States; Albert K. Smiley of Redlands fame; John Burroughs and Bishop William Lawrence of Massachusetts; and David Starr Jordan, President of Stanford University, all played major roles in the proceedings.[5]

Frank Miller opened the meeting informally by presenting music from the Music Room's new grand organ. Miller used the occasion to dedicate the cathedral organ played by John McClellan, organist of the Mormon Tabernacle at Salt Lake City.

Dr. Jordan, Frank Miller's good friend presided, introducing prominent speakers and reading communications from President William Howard Taft and Andrew Carnegie. Mayor Samuel Cary Evans, Riverside's first elected mayor, presented a unique silk banner to Dr. Jordan, a copy of the flag planted by Peary at the North Pole. It bore stars and stripes upon a white field with the words, "Peace For All Nations," and represented a worldwide symbolic flag advocating peace. Teachers were guests of Frank Miller and school children were dismissed early to attend Dr. Jordan's afternoon session.

Dignitaries spoke on the horrors of war, a common theme expressed by prominent citizens and men of the church. Each urged America to take the lead position in bringing about universal peace. At the conclusion of the conference, the audience agreed to work for peace and 300 people joined the Riverside Peace Society, naming Frank Miller president and Matthew Gage vice-president.

During the week of the Peace Conference, Cornelius Rumsey passed away at the Loma Linda Sanitarium where he was receiving treatments for "a slight shock of paralysis." His death was mourned by citizens who praised his generous contributions and personal services to the community.[6] Matthew attended Mr. Rumsey's services at Calvary Presbyterian Church, where he reflected that they both were born in the same year. At age 67, Matthew Gage had become a congenial, mellow citizen and a citrus grower occasionally referred to as the famous canal builder. He was credited for Riverside's beautiful citrus groves and flourishing industry.

Later in 1911, Matthew read in the newspaper that Otto Newman had died in Los Angeles. He had been an adversary, struggling to claim a portion of Section 30. Sixty-four-year-old Otto never married and, as the brother of Frank Miller's son-in-law, he became a member of Frank Miller's household. Accordingly, his services were held in the Miller's private parlors of the Mission Inn and he was buried in Evergreen Cemetery.

Matthew had sold several lots in Section 30 fronting on Eighth Street where commercial enterprises were developing. This main road from downtown Riverside had been improved and extended over the Box Springs grade to Alessandro, a farming community. Matthew's previous sales did not reduce his debts in the form of lawyer's fees and delinquent notes. His daughter, Maude, and her son Gage Henderson, returned to the family home after Maude divorced her husband, Henry Henderson.[7] In spite of domestic and financial difficulties, the Gage household was filled with music and good literature and a safe refuge from legal proceedings and courtroom encounters. Matthew and Jane had many friends, some from church, others connected to the citrus business and the aging couple continued to experience a warm community relationship.

Three hundred citizens were invited to Ethan Allen Chase's 80th birthday party on January 19, 1912. Matthew, one of the honored guests, traveled to the great Chase Ranch in Corona to take part in the lavish banquet commemorating a man he admired and called a friend. The new Chase packinghouse, the appropriate site for the party, was decorated with palm branches and greenery and decorative screens shielding the newly installed commercial equipment. Local high school girls cheerfully worked as waitresses, serving the long tables covered with white tablecloths.

Harry Chase, as toastmaster, introduced a long list of speakers who each highlighted Chase's accomplishments. Mayor William Peters commented:

> Ethan Allen Chase was past 60 years old when he came to Riverside. He liked the climate, he liked the county, and he liked the people, and recognized possibilities of fruit growing here. He invested his capital in business with his sons and he has become the largest, most successful fruit grower in the state.[8]

The large assembly sang "Happy Birthday" as a happy, alert Ethan Allen Chase smiled with delight to be so honored.

Members of the Calvary Presbyterian Church gathered on June 19, 1912, to celebrate the Twenty-Fifth Anniversary of the founding of their church. The Silver Anniversary began with a receiving line composed of prominent church members including Margaret, Jane and Matthew Gage, all charter members. Throughout the church parlors and vestibules were large bouquets of white flowers to symbolize the color silver and bouquets of Shasta daisies and white carnations complemented the silver theme.

A photograph gallery had been assembled displaying pictures of former members and past pastors of the church. A large portrait of Margaret Orr Gage, Matthew's mother, held a place of honor framed in beautiful clusters of magnolia blossoms. Old and new members of the church gathered

Ethan Allen Chase

around the gallery recognizing family members and friends who had participated in church activities throughout the years.[9]

The Gages, and others in the receiving line, were seated on a small platform near the front of the church. Former choir members, including Matthew's daughter Margaret, and his brother John Gage, took places in the choir loft as former organist Lilla Irving Mylne started the program with her organ music. After a selection of hymns accompanied by the choir, Dr. Hunter addressed the assembled charter members.

> I do not wonder that when you people set out to build a church that you did it well, for you are men and women of vision. You charter members will go down in history as founding a great church.[10]

Church historian, A. A. Adair, recalled events in founding the church and expressed his deep gratitude to Matthew and Jane Gage for having presented a much appreciated organ to the church. Matthew Gage was introduced as one of the most prominent of the charter members, a founder of the church, and was asked to say a few words.

> When a noble few, a band of brothers and sisters, who were instrumental in founding this church commenced their work, they looked forward, not backward.

Matthew Gage eulogized past members and pastors who had worked to establish the successful church. He was pleased to introduce his 42-year-old daughter, Margaret, who sang "Open Thou Mine Eyes" in a pleasant soprano voice.[11]

Congratulatory communications from former members were read including hardy greetings from former elder, Robert Gage. He was living in Utica, New York and was remembered for his stable influence in church affairs. The celebration moved outdoors where Japanese lanterns brightened the flourishing garden and everyone enjoyed the old-fashioned get-together with ice cream and cake.

During the summer, Riverside's Board of Health issued a proclamation forbidding any gathering of children under 15-years-of-age due to an epidemic of infantile paralysis. The dreaded disease had infected children throughout the county and Matthew and Jane were concerned about Gage Henderson, their seven-year-old grandson. However, when the black wreath of death appeared on the Gage's front door that fall, it announced the death of their youngest child, Katherine MacKenzie Gage, age 23 years, from tuberculosis.[12] She had been in declining health throughout the summer and steadily grew weaker and weaker. She was buried in Olivewood Cemetery next to her siblings and grandmother. Matthew and Jane turned to their church for comfort and solace where a solicitous congregation helped the bereaved couple once again.

The Gages frequently attended church gatherings and civic affairs where conversations often turned to scandalous local news and disturbing events. Riverside was not free of crime and innocent people were being hurt and killed. Judge Holton Webb had been shot after sentencing a prisoner. An Arlington police officer was killed while on duty and house robberies were common occurrences. Sheriff Frank Wilson traveled to Texas and purchased three bloodhounds to help fight crime. In September, Chief of Police Philip Coburn raided the Victoria Club, a private country club, and arrested personnel for serving liquor to non-members.[13]

Churches in Riverside were continuing their campaign against saloons as they stressed abstinence from liquor. Regardless of sermons stressing righteous behavior and the evils of liquor, an embarrassing scandal shocked officials and citizens throughout the state. On December 11, 1912, John Baird, acting police chief, was shot and killed by Bert Barnett, a fellow officer on duty, who was "under the influence of alcohol."[14] News of the sensational murder by a drunken policeman spread from one household to another. The Gage family could not comprehend such aggressive, dubious

Matthew Gage

behavior by Bert Barnett, a good family man with four lovely children.

As the story unfolded, Philip M. Coburn had been appointed police chief the first of the year by William L.

Peters, the new incoming mayor. Mayor Peters began a vigorous campaign against "demon whiskey" and Chief Coburn and Deputy Chief John Baird set out to enforce local ordinances forbidding alcohol sales within the city limits. The City Council passed a resolution, "The man who violates the law must suffer the penalty."[15]

When Coburn became ill in November, 33-year-old John Baird filled his position as acting chief and managed the six-man squad. Coburn died December 8. Late Saturday night, December 12, Patrolman Bert Barrett and John Baird went to the Star Rooming House on Eighth Street where a fight had been reported. Finding no one responsible for the commotion, Baird returned to the two-room station in the Loring Building on Seventh Street and left Barrett at the rooming house where opened bottles of whiskey remained.

After they rejoined each other at the station, Chief Baird accused Barrett of drinking while on duty. The two swore at each other, then became physical, and were pulled apart by another officer on duty. It was after midnight when Barrett fired three bullets into John Baird, who died on the floor of police headquarters.

Mayor Peters rushed to the police station and tried to unravel the strange turn of events. It was difficult to conceive that a reputable man such as Bert Barrett, sworn to uphold the law, had killed his superior officer in a fit of passion caused by whiskey. Barrett went to jail where he remained during John Baird's funeral. It took place one week, to the hour, after Philip Coburn's funeral. Bert Barrett's murder trial was postponed until April 1913, when he testified in his own defense. The jury found him guilty of manslaughter and sentenced him to ten years in San Quentin.[16]

City officials recognized that they had big problems when shipments of liquor regularly appeared in Riverside. Mayor William Peters stressed the seriousness of the problem when he covered the table used by City Council members with evidence.

The Council Chambers appeared to be a wholesale liquor house with 49 flasks of various sizes, ranging from half pints to quarts, bottles of beer and small bottles of mixed cocktails. The mayor revoked the liquor permits of four drug stores and one hotel. He had been secretly informed that two city policemen had been suspected of tipping off druggists, or owners of blind pigs, before a raid. Blind pigs were hidden liquor stashes. No one denied the Mayor's suspicion.

Less than a week after John Baird was shot, Corona City Marshall Alexander was killed by "thugs" who lured him from his home and shot him twice. Bootleggers were suspected. The Prohibition Alliance, backed by Matthew Gage and the mayor, worked to clear the city of illegal bootleggers.[17] While Barrett was waiting trial in the Riverside County jail, Chief of Police Corrington reported a quiet New Year's Eve.

The next morning many Riversiders boarded a special *Southern Pacific* train for Pasadena's Tournament of Roses. The parade featured aviator Galvarth Rogers who showered perfumed carnations from a high altitude as spectators scrambled for souvenirs.[18] Cars and carriages covered in fresh flowers paraded down the boulevard as the crowd cheered.

January 1, 1913, was also the day when Riverside City Hall officially moved from the Loring Building into larger quarters in the Reynolds Block at Ninth and Orange streets. The city leased 18 rooms on the second floor with offices for the mayor, city engineer, street department, building inspector and council rooms. The police department moved into a separate building on Ninth Street, located between the alley and Orange Street. The city paid $150 a month for the leased space.[19]

Rather than move the confiscated illegal liquor to the new facility, the police force emptied gallons and gallons of rot gut, white mule and home brew into the gutter in front of the old police station on Seventh Street near Main Street.[20] As the contraband liquid slowly flowed into the storm drain, strong fumes spread through the Glenwood Mission Inn where guests were perplexed by the strange odor.

A few days later, Riverside was confronted with cold temperatures and a sky filled with smudge. December had been one of the driest in history and Charlie Hatfield made his annual offer to bring 10-to-30 inches of rain by the middle of April. Many citrus growers in Riverside would have gratefully paid his fee if they had foreseen what historically became known as the big freeze of 1913.

CHAPTER 13

Cold weather and a biting wind kept most people indoors on Sunday, January 6 with the highest temperature only 45 degrees. At sunset the wind subsided and, by 7 o'clock, Matthew received a telephone call from the foreman of the National Orange Company packinghouse. Citrus groves in Matthew's Section 30 were cared for by the packinghouse owned by Ethan Allen Chase and his sons, Harry and Frank. A night rider, employed by the company, checked strategically placed thermometers in selected groves and alerted growers as temperatures declined. This was the earliest hour Matthew had ever been summoned.

A previous weather forecast called for normal temperatures during the remaining days of the season. It

Citrus Groves in Arlington Heights

was generally accepted that most frost damage occurred in December and before January 5. This was based on past weather records and a rule of thumb among farmers. Cool nights were beneficial to navel oranges, enhancing color and flavor but when temperatures dropped below freezing growers took to frost protection measures. Frozen fruit was not marketable.[1]

On Sunday night temperatures dropped to 22 degrees and packinghouses throughout southern California summoned employees to the groves. Priestley Hall burned wet straw placed over screened pans of coal to heat the air, while other growers resorted to any means available to keep crops from freezing.

Cold north winds blew over hillsides of citrus before sweeping down into the valleys. This cold flow of air seriously injured trees growing on high ground that had never before required frost protection. In certain localities temperatures remained below freezing for nearly 60 hours. Bark split on mature trees and frozen oranges and lemons fell to the ground.[2]

On Monday a cold northern wind blew all day and after sunset temperatures dropped quickly, reaching a low of 22 degrees. This weather system, straight from Alaska and northwestern Canada, reached as far south as San Diego and brought a surge of artic air behind it. All activities in Riverside were cancelled and schools remained closed. Air, filled with particles of soot from burning smudge pots of crude oil, was unfit to breathe. People were forced to remain indoors for several days.

Citrus growers, including Matthew, considered smudging effective and the best means of frost protection. Trouble came when growers were unprepared or thought that their groves were located in frost-free areas on high ground. Unfortunately, many found their suppositions to be inaccurate and suffered severe damage.

On Monday night the Arlington Heights Fruit Company had 200 men firing 150,000 pots.[3] Dispatchers for *Southern*

Pacific and Santa Fe and Salt Lake Railroads worked around the clock delivering crude oil in cars that carried 12,000 gallons each. Railroad companies realized that saving citrus crops would promote future freight traffic and good relations with growers.

Cold, windy weather was responsible for snapping and breaking telephone wires and electric light poles. Midday winds uprooted trees, cracked limbs and whipped fruit from branches. People thought Riverside was experiencing a miniature blizzard and a Weather Bureau bulletin alerted citizens to protect their livestock.

A freezing wind storm produced high tides and choppy seas, forcing ships to head for safe harbors. Nevertheless, three vessels were swept ashore by raging water and destroyed, killing seven seamen.[4] Frozen pipes burst in homes, offices and public buildings throughout southern California and plumbers were busy for weeks.

Hills near San Francisco were covered in snow and trolley cars in Los Angeles could not operate due to frozen air-brake valves. In Portland, milk delivered on doorsteps became solid chunks of ice. Denver reported 31 degrees below zero. Local baseball games were cancelled, the Casa Blanca Tennis tournament was called off and the grand opening of the new Hotel Tetley had few visitors. Mission Inn guests were content to remain indoors where whist parties and afternoon teas were instantly planned to entertain confined guests.

A work-crew from the National Orange Company kept smudge pots glowing in Section 30, where Matthew had several hundred acres of navel trees. He inspected the operation each night, but did not linger as the experienced crew went to work. Sixty-nine-year-old Matthew did not relish spending nights outdoors in freezing weather.

During the period of the big freeze, church congregations met daily and prayed for rain and warmer weather. One pastor told his flock:

Results of the 1913 Big Freeze

There are two theories as to who sent the freeze. Some claimed Satan caused this terrible calamity. Others hold that our God has quietly laid his hand upon us to save us in our mad dash for money and pleasure from eternal destruction. These are surely times that try men's souls.[5]

Another church issue surfaced when growers irrigated on Sundays, prompting lively discussions and hot debates. Growers stressed that it was necessary to irrigate when water was scheduled, regardless of the day of the week. One old timer maintained "there should be less effort put on faith and more use of the shovel whenever water entered the canals."

After four nights of below freezing temperatures, rain began to fall on January 9. Timing of the storm was opportune as showers broke the cold spell and could ultimately restore the trees back to normal. The long drought that had brought just 1.38 inches to Riverside since June and 1.23 inches to Los Angeles was broken.[6] Only time would tell if any fruit remained marketable.

Agricultural inspectors were quickly sent to ensure that packinghouse procedures were adequate to prevent the marketing of frozen fruit. While most packers were cautious and diligent, some were not and the inspections were necessary to minimize or eliminate the shipment of sub-par fruit to eastern markets. Quality fruit was imperative if the Riverside navel orange was to retain its world-class reputation.

Although it was difficult to distinguish between a frozen orange and a sound one, Ethan Allen Chase's son, Frank, came up with a simple test to separate them.[7] Since frozen fruit dries out, it is lighter and therefore it will rise to the surface in a tank of water, while sound fruit sinks to the bottom. Functional equipment was subsequently developed and made available to all packinghouses through the generosity of Frank Chase.

The shipment of frozen fruit was forbidden by the Federal Board of Food and Drugs, however packinghouses were permitted to ship lesser damaged fruit in boxes clearly labeled: Damaged By Frost.

In February, William H. Winterbotham of London and his son Fred, came to inspect the Riverside Trust Company property in Arlington Heights. The senior Mr. Winterbotham was a member of the prestigious Price Waterhouse & Company and both father and son were solicitors. William Fraser had contacted the Riverside Trust Company in England requesting a member of the board of directors to inspect damage caused by the big freeze. William Winterbotham had served the royal government in legal matters and was a director.

Reports had reached London claiming that thousands of acres of citrus in Arlington Heights had been destroyed by the big freeze. After Mr. Winterbotham and his son settled in the Mission Inn, he began daily inspections of citrus groves owned by the Trust Company.[8] They stayed for three weeks observing packinghouse procedures and sought amplification of the "doctrine of optimism for the citrus industry."[9]

Dr. Herbert John Webber, professor at Cornell University, had been appointed director of Riverside's Citrus Experiment Station located at the base of Mount Rubidoux. He took charge of the station in January 1913 during what remains the most devastating freeze on record. He advised horticulturists to leave injured trees alone for four to six months before pruning.[10] Citrus growers throughout southern California were concerned about their crops, trees and the future of the industry.

Speakers at the Riverside Businessmen's annual banquet, held in the Mission Inn, praised growers for withholding shipments of questionable fruit in order to retain Riverside's fine reputation.[11] Matthew Gage was anxious to know if his trees in Section 30 would survive the devastating freeze, noting that his neighbor's grove resembled the aftermath of a giant fireball. It was a time of transition for many farm families as they left Riverside in search of greener pastures.

William Gage Irving was Riverside's City Attorney in 1913. That February, he married Maude Gage Henderson. Matthew and Jane accompanied the couple to Los Angeles, where a simple ceremony took place in the courthouse.[12] There was little fanfare, in part because they were first cousins. Nevertheless, William and Maude and her son, Gage Henderson, who later took the name Irving, became a popular family, highly regarded in the community. The

William Irvings lived with the Gage family for some time and Matthew was delighted to have the youthful companionship of his only grandchild.

The year 1913 was an election year and early in May a general debate surfaced as to who would be the most likely candidate for the office of mayor in the November election. Petitions were circulated on behalf of William Gage Irving as a non-partisan candidate. When news spread that Mr. Irving agreed to run, his office was besieged with congratulatory telephone calls. Attorneys and businessmen gathered signatures, convinced that he would be a responsible mayor.[13] Later, William Irving dropped out of the race for mayor because his extensive law practice involved difficult water litigation throughout the state. Oscar Ford was elected Mayor of Riverside later that year.

Matthew hired a crew of well diggers to search for water in the northwest corner of Section 30 and, to everyone's surprise, they struck water on May 15, 1913. The water flowed profusely with a capacity to irrigate 450 acres. It was estimated to be worth $95,000 with 95 to 100 inches at $1,000 an inch.[14] Matthew still owned 365 acres in Section 30 and had not yet decided if he would plant or sell the land and water to a syndicate. Friends and neighbors wondered how different Matthew's life might have been altered if he had discovered this unknown water source in 1882 after filing to reclaim Section 30.

John Henry Reed invited one hundred distinguished guests to his 80th birthday party in June 1913 including his friend, Matthew Gage. The gathering assembled in the Mission Inn to pay tribute to Reed, the former City Tree Warden who was largely responsible for making Riverside a city of trees. The office of Tree Warden had been created in 1906 for the purpose of planting and caring for trees along city streets. There were many speeches including Mr. Reed's address:

> When we first took up citrus farming, we found it was not the simple thing it had looked to be in print. I asked

neighbors to come and talk over problems so we could learn from one another and the first horticulturist club in the state was organized in my little cottage. The Riverside Horticulturist Club helped improve orchard methods and through its influence we reached recognition from state and national departments.

Riverside is approaching the most important crisis in its history - we are liable to lose distinction of our most valuable asset. The bill providing for the extension of the citrus experiment station and post-graduate school, signed by the Governor yesterday, settles the matter of its coming existence. Riverside is the logical place and is liable to lose the prize. Other desirable locations are planning to secure the station but we cannot afford to lose. The school will add 5-to 10-percent value to every acre of farm land in the vicinity.

Now, like a loyal octogenarian, I will get on the shelf and pull the curtain down. But I give you fair warning, I shall keep a peep hole open and if you folks don't work hard for maintaining Riverside's rightful place as the citrus center and the city beautiful, you will hear from me.[15]

J. H. Reed had been instrumental in establishing the University of California Citrus Station in Riverside in 1906. Located on 20 acres at the foot of Mount Rubidoux, an experimental orchard was developed where tests on tree nutrition and frost protection were performed. After the big freeze of 1913, the station was deemed inadequate and undersized. Citrus growers, with the support of the California Fruit Growers Exchange, began a vigorous campaign for a larger experiment station and research center.

Ethan Allen Chase invited college professors to Riverside to express their views on the future of the citrus industry. One speaker reported:

Matthew and Jane wth grandson Gage Henderson

The most encouraging sign is the cooperation of the state educational institutions with agriculturists.

The citrus market became depressed from panic shipments of damaged fruit and the loss of thousands of acres of dead trees presented a gloomy future. The 1913 state legislature provided the Regents of the University of California $60,000 to purchase land for a new citrus experiment station and authorized the regents to select the site. When the bill was introduced, it was understood that the City of Riverside would retain the station and move onto a new site. On June 9,

1913, however, the state legislature provided additional funds for the acquisition of land and water rights for a new station to be established in one of the seven southern California counties.[16] Thus Los Angeles County began a campaign to locate the new station in the San Fernando Valley and strongly opposed placing the station in Riverside.

While Riverside sought to gain support for the experiment station, Matthew was saddened to hear of Judge Joseph Noyes' passing. The superior court judge had always treated him fairly. After 12 years on the bench, Noyes retired to Los Angeles to be near his grown children after his wife died. Grieving over her death, the judge went to Sycamore Park with a book, leaned against a giant oak tree, and consumed a small bottle of laudanum. A note, used as a bookmark, explained his grief and final actions.

Riverside's Chamber of Commerce worked on behalf of the community to retain the experiment station. After the governor announced the seven counties eligible for the new experiment station, 60 potential sites were submitted. The regents appointed a search committee that ultimately eliminated from consideration all but three sites, San Fernando, Pomona and Riverside.

Boosters for the experiment station, including Riverside's Chamber of Commerce members, organized to determine the best possible location for a new station. Expansion of the existing Mount Rubidoux station was not plausible with limited available land due to the adjoining Evergreen Cemetery and the proximity of Chinatown. The Arlington district emerged as too far from downtown and land in Arlington Heights was too costly.

The committee agreed on a stretch of rural land located two-and-a-half miles east of the center of town near the Box Springs grade road, including part of Section 30. It consisted of 407 acres containing 236 acres of fine, uniform soil, 62 acres of foothill property and 109 acres of rolling land for future building sites. Significant water was available from the Gage Canal and a free flowing well, with the capacity of irrigating the entire tract. The city agreed to furnish electricity to the new station at a reduced rate, the lowest ever charged for irrigation purposes.

The proposed site had a frontage of 7,000 feet on both sides of Box Springs grade road, the inland boulevard connecting Los Angeles and San Diego. A new enterprise known as the Riverside Autobus Company was ready to offer transportation from the Santa Fe train depot to the site of the proposed new station.

Riverside's chamber members, citrus growers, and the California Fruit Growers Exchange signed agreements to financially assist in acquiring lands that exceeded the state's allotment. If options on lands for the proposed site exceeded the state's appropriation, orange growers agreed to underwrite $8,000, to be raised by an assessment of half-a-cent a box on fruit shipped in the 1914-15 and 1915-16 seasons.[17] The Chamber also agreed to contribute $18,000 from member and community donations.

Officers of the Riverside committee, Chairman Samuel C. Evans, Ethan Allen Chase and John H. Reed submitted a proposal to the three regents who were investigating each site. When the regents inspected the Riverside site, containing 407 acres, they spent less than 40 minutes evaluating the property.[18] Their reports, supposedly confidential documents, became public information in Los Angeles newspapers. Regents asserted Riverside's site contained poor soil and infested orchards. Riverside quickly disputed these false claims and the Chamber of Commerce committee increased the proposed tract by 200 acres.

Los Angeles newspapers campaigned for the San Fernando site and inferred that Riverside's location was too remote. On November 5, 1913, 30,000 people gathered in the San Fernando Valley, northwest of Los Angeles, to witness the first flow of water from the Owens Valley-Los Angeles Aqueduct. Influential men and powerful interests were speculating that San Fernando would become the citrus capital of California. Chairman Samuel C. Evans said, "big business backing for San Fernando is the hardest thing for the committee to fight."[19]

Riverside citrus station boosters traveled throughout southern California covering hundreds of miles in an effort to get support and to fight the San Fernando contingent. San Diego and other counties joined in the drive to retain the Riverside station, where a graduate school for studies of sub-tropical agriculture could eventually be established.

During the struggle of the site selection, Dr. H. J. Webber declined to express his preference. He did, however, compliment Riverside's committee on its community support and the interest that it had generated. The town was indeed proud of its growing citrus industry.

CHAPTER 14

A committee of three regents, two of whom favored San Fernando and one Riverside, was appointed to investigate the two most preferred sites. Samuel C. Evans, chairman of the Riverside Chamber of Commerce site committee, announced that 70 acres had been added to Riverside's offer, making a total of 471 acres. The University of California would obtain land and water rights valued at $137,025.[1]

On December 8, 1914, the Board of Regents met in San Francisco to select the site for the new experiment station. Riverside, ever optimistic, announced that the curfew whistle would blast signaling victory for the town.

At the last minute, however, Pomona came forward with a promising proposition for the Board to consider, resulting in postponement of a decision until December 22. Mr. Evans and the Riverside

Samuel C. Evans

211

delegation came home for a week, before returning to San Francisco. On December 22, San Fernando representatives presented their case, displaying enlarged photographs of their proposed site. Samuel Evans then spoke in behalf of Riverside's offer, stating that citrus growers throughout southern California preferred keeping the station in Riverside where its central location would most directly serve southern California horticulturists.

When 18 regents retired into an executive session, they debated the pros and cons of each location, with heated discussions lasting over three hours. One regent refused to have anything to do with the selection of a location and was not present for the final vote. It was presumed that he had a conflict of interest and removed himself from voting. While mixed arguments took place in the executive session, citizens in Riverside anxiously awaited the outcome. The final vote came to 14 regents favoring Riverside and four for San Fernando.[2] Several regents living near Los Angeles, whose personal interests would be materially advanced by the selection of San Fernando, voted for Riverside without reservation.

News of the victory reached the city by telegram and the long-awaited happy announcement spread rapidly across town. Matthew Gage knew of the successful outcome when he heard the loud power plant whistle and clanging bells from the Mission Inn. The small town of Riverside, with a population of 16,500, celebrated its selection after months of work. The University's acquisition of 80 acres in Section 30 pleased Matthew as he realized the importance of establishing an expanding experiment station located in the heart of the citrus industry. Riverside's prestige as the citrus capital of California would finally be acknowledged upon completion of the University's facilities.

Members of the chamber committee, who attended the regent's meeting, returned to Los Angeles on the "Owl" train and by car to Riverside. That evening, following the celebration whistles, there were 1,000 telephone calls seeking information on the outcome of the regents meeting. Bold headlines the next day announced Riverside's victory, with much credit given to Samuel C. Evans and his hard working chamber of commerce committee. Riverside received a welcome Christmas present as the beneficiary of the university's selection.[3]

Governor Johnson was satisfied that the citrus station matter was settled effectively and justly. Members of the chamber committee continued to work until all funds were received and deeds recorded. Letters of appreciation were sent to citrus communities and organizations, to boards of supervisors and to newspaper editors who had helped make Riverside's campaign a success.

The university received 471 acres for $55,000. Good citrus land was valued at $350 an acre and Matthew received $28,000 on June 23, 1915 when the Regents of the University of California recorded deeds to 80 acres of Section 30.[4] The land was located near the center of the section, contiguous to other University acquisitions.

Cost of the entire transaction was $18,400 in excess of the state allotment. Citizens of Riverside, neighboring citrus communities, and chamber members who had supported the citrus station honored their pledges. President Gennett, of the Orange Land Investment Company of Los Angeles, reduced the cost of his company's land by $10,000, considering it a donation to Riverside and the University of California.[5]

By March, the University of California Regents selected architect Lester Hibbard of Los Angeles to design the buildings for the experiment station. His plans for the central laboratory building reflected a Mission Revival style of architecture, with large wings extending from either end. Dr. Webber worked with Hubbard in designing floor plans to provide efficiency in agricultural experiments.[6] World War I caused delays in materials and labor, so the building was not officially dedicated until 1918.

World War I began in the summer of 1914 and Great Britain declared war against Germany that August. Church missionaries, sent to distressed countries, reported

Matthew and Jane Gage

gruesome stories of terrible battles and inhumane conduct. Congregations across the United States learned of the horrors of war and a strong Christian peace movement evolved. Reverend W. A. Hunter of Riverside's Calvary Presbyterian Church, denounced all aspects of war and Matthew Gage supported the goal of the peace movement to put an end to all wars.[7] At a meeting in February 1915, the Riverside Peace

Society was reorganized with Frank Miller as president and Matthew Gage as vice-president.

Prominent speakers presented bold resolutions, advocating friendly pacts with neutral nations to live in peace "without forts or battleships." One speaker theorized that a new era of civilization could be created, whereby disputes between nations would be settled by properly constituted courts of law rather than brute force. Three hundred people joined the Riverside Peace Society in one day.[8]

Matthew continued to keep abreast of activities in Arlington Heights although he no longer had any vested interest. The Gage Canal Company was building a huge dam at the mouth of Mockingbird Canyon in Arlington Heights for storage of winter rains. The ambitious project started in 1911 but was delayed for several years due to adverse weather. The immense reservoir, nearly a mile wide, appeared to be a peaceful lake except for an array of nozzles, pumps and hydraulic equipment attached to a section of its shoreline.[9] Matthew recalled the days when surveyors relied on the contour of land for gravity flow.

After Matthew received payment from the regents for his land in Section 30, he and Jane traveled to Canada to visit family and friends. Jane's sisters and Matthew's sister, Sarah Spooner, were living in Ontario. The couple planned to spend several months there and then continue on to England and Ireland for the summer to avoid Riverside's heat. World War I was escalating, however, and they remained in Canada until early fall. The sinking of the British liner *Lusitania* by a German submarine on May 7, 1915, reminded them of the hazards associated with the unrest in Europe.

Matthew's last public appearance was in November 1915 to honor his long-time friend Frank Miller. The Wednesday Morning Club had organized a grand reception in recognition of Mr. Miller's many contributions to "the furtherance of art in the city of Riverside." The festive occasion was endorsed by individuals and civic organizations throughout the city.

Frank and Marion Miller, returning from an extended eastern trip, were unaware of the planned festivities.[10]

On November 6 friends and neighbors gathered in the Mission Inn's beautifully decorated Music Room where Matthew Gage stood in the receiving line with William G. Irving, J. H. Reed, Samuel C. Evans and other prominent dignitaries. Five hundred guests filled the lavish room where distinguished speakers paid tribute to Frank Miller for his many achievements in beautifying Riverside.

One speaker noted that Mr. Miller's Mission Revival style of architecture had served as a model for the Pan American Exposition in San Francisco, while another offered to endorse Frank Miller "for president of the United States." "If the honoree declared his intention to build a bridge across the Pacific Ocean, I would start selling tickets tomorrow morning," said a close friend.[11] Frank Miller expressed his heartfelt thanks to the community and was presented with a gold watch in appreciation for his philanthropic interest in the city. Mr. Miller stated that the best part of his recent eastern trip was coming home to Riverside.

On Christmas Eve, under a cloudless sky, Riverside's community Christmas tree came to life as thousands of spectators watched the lighting of the tree in White Park. The decorative tree with its colored electric lights, together with holiday music by three bands, beautifully captured the spirit of Christmas. Christmas Day turned cold and windy as a fierce sand and wind storm forced people to remain indoors and many holiday travelers were stranded.

The disagreeable weather brought heavy rainfall and snow to higher elevations. Towns throughout Riverside County experienced the heaviest snowstorm since 1882. Matthew and Jane were content to spend the holiday near their warm fireplace.

Rain continued to fall intermittently for days causing the Santa Ana River to overflow its boundaries. The bridge to Los Angeles collapsed from the force of the deluge, isolating Riverside once again. The force of the water knocked out dykes and canals and undermined railroad tracks. The lake at Fairmount Park overflowed and transportation in town ceased as trolley cars were forced out of service.[12]

The cold, damp weather took its toll on Matthew Gage who developed a cold and was forced to remain in his home. As his cold worsened, his doctor ordered him to bed and suspected that he had developed pneumonia. Jane filled his room with vapors to ease his breathing and family members visited often. In spite of Jane's loving care, Matthew Gage, age 72, died shortly after midnight on Saturday, January 22, 1916.[13]

His death saddened the community. Newspapers praised his many achievements, including the building of the Gage Canal. Simple funeral services were held Monday morning in Calvary Presbyterian Church. The building at Ninth and Lime filled with old friends and neighbors who came to pay their respects. His ornate bier was hidden beneath layers of floral tributes. Pall bearers included family members John Gage, Robert Irving, John Mylne, William G. Irving, E. W. Trevelyan and Norman Irving.

Music, so much a part of Matthew's life, was rendered by Mr. Hopkins at the organ donated by Jane Gage in memory of their departed children.[14] The emotional Mendelssohn's Funeral March brought tears to the mourners.

Reverend W. A. Hunter spoke of Matthew's religious life, his simple faith, and a heart free of bitterness. The minister of the Magnolia Avenue Presbyterian Church recalled the family's early association and generous gift of a fine clock to that church. A list of dignitaries acknowledged Matthew Gage's many accomplishments and his contributions to the city of Riverside. One speaker described Mr. Gage as a rare combination of intellect and tireless energy, who had worked for the betterment of the community without seeking personal gain or reward. A friend recalled that Matthew had crossed the Atlantic Ocean 29 times and thought it might be a record. He confessed that he would miss his close companion who always had a ready smile and good sense of humor.

Mayor Oscar Ford expressed "appreciation of the man who brought great personal qualities to the city by his abilities of leadership, powers to conceive and perform great things. He had ability to accomplish notable deeds in the face of adversity and discouragement and this reflected on his sterling character."[15]

The eulogy focused on Matthew's survivors, his wife Jane, daughters Margaret, Anna, and Maude, grandson Gage (Henderson) Irving, sisters Eliza Gage Irving and Sarah Spooner and brothers John and Robert.

After the Monday morning service, Matthew Gage's body was transferred to Los Angeles on the noon train to be cremated.[16] Facilities in Evergreen Cemetery's new Mausoleum were not fully completed and the closest crematorium was in Los Angeles. The *Santa Fe Railroad* had announced that trains would not move until the rain ceased. Monday, however, proved to be a dry day and the train ran on schedule.

The following week the Riverside Chamber of Commerce passed a resolution in appreciation of Matthew Gage's work:

> Resolved that the directors of the Riverside Chamber of Commerce record their sincere regret at the death of Matthew Gage, Riverside pioneer and creator of the water system that bears his name.[17]

Ethan Allen Chase wrote an article recalling his long admiration of Matthew Gage and his accomplishments. He stated:

> Of all the men who have lived, no one has contributed so much to the making of Riverside as Matthew Gage. His work shall live in history and his name will be indelibly written in the hearts of grateful people.[18]

The Gage House Covered in Rose Bushes

Two weeks after Matthew's death, Jane received an official notice to vacate the Fourteenth Street house by March 1 or before. Matthew's life interest in the property terminated upon his death and the bank reclaimed its legal property. After 35 years in the Fourteenth Street house, Jane, Margaret and Anna had to move.

As executrix of Matthew's estate, Jane inherited his assets and his debts. Matthew's bank account totaled $1,720 and his farm equipment, including two mules and a horse named Peter, sold for $2,600. He owned one share of capital stock in the Victoria Club, Certificate Number 44, valued at $50. His largest asset was 300 acres in Section 30, valued at $300 an acre. The appraised value of his entire estate was estimated to be $94,000.[19]

Matthew's many debts included a $25,000 mortgage against Section 30, unpaid notes, delinquent tax fees and penalties, lawyer fees and personal debts that reduced the estate to less than $20,000. Margaret, Anna, and Maude each received a token remembrance of $10.

Jane purchased a modest six room house on New Magnolia Avenue near Rosewood Place and the new Magnolia Elementary School.[20] It was conveniently located, with the Magnolia Avenue streetcar only a few steps away. The following year, Anna Gage became engaged to Henry Schuyler Montgomery and the young couple planned to marry in December 1917. Their wedding was postponed when Henry received a wartime commission as an Army engineer and immediately reported to training camp. Anna continued working as a stenographer for the law firm of McFarland & Irving. In September 1918, the couple was married in a quiet ceremony in Jane's home, with Dr. W. A. Hunter of Calvary Presbyterian Church officiating.[21] After his military service, Henry became a competent mining engineer and the couple settled in Pasadena.

The University of California Experiment Station and School of Tropical Agriculture was dedicated on a beautiful spring day in March 1918. The attractive two-story administration building featured a main wing and basement with construction of a second wing postponed until after World War I. There were efforts to include an agricultural school with the new station similar to the University of California, Davis.

After the war, in 1920, Regents of the University of California appropriated $141,000 to purchase additional land to enlarge the Citrus Experiment Station and to develop a farm school. Governor William D. Stephens signed the contract to purchase 300 acres at $300 per acre in the Gage Tract, 80 acres of adjacent land planted in orange groves at $300 per acre, and water rights from the Gage Canal not to exceed $900 per inch or $40,500.[22]

Jane Gage sold the last parcels of Matthew's Section 30 to the Regents of the University of California. After 38 years of turmoil and aggravation, the coveted Section 30 no longer belonged to a Gage family member.

In 1928, Margaret Jane Gage, eldest daughter of Matthew and Jane, died of tuberculosis at the age of 58. She had been Jane's constant companion since their arrival in Riverside in 1881. She was cremated and her ashes were interred in Olivewood Cemetery the following year.[23] Jane now relied on her daughter, Maude, her son-in-law William Gage Irving, and her grandson Gage for assistance whenever necessary.

On April 1, 1929, William and Maude Irving escorted Jane to a special memorial presentation at the Riverside Public Library. Head librarian Charles Wood and Harry Chase greeted guests for a heart-warming ceremony honoring Matthew Gage. Seventy-three-year-old Harry Chase presented an impressive, two-foot-high bronze bust of Matthew Gage to the public library. It had been created by Julia Wendt of Los Angeles and depicted Matthew in his middle years. Spectators, and invited guests, considered it a "splendid likeness." The inscription at the base read: "Matthew Gage, Canal Builder Presented to the Riverside Public Library by the family of Ethan Allen Chase." Harry Chase informed the audience it would be placed in a choice location for the public to admire and concluded with this tribute:

> The Chase family takes pleasure in presenting to the library a bust of Matthew Gage. The library is permanent and in our opinion the proper custodian of all things concerned with the history of Riverside. When a city is in the making, everybody is interested in everything. But as time goes on, pioneers pass on and newcomers are accustomed to public works that were the very cornerstones of the entire community.
> It is with this thought in mind that we wish to do what is possible to help perpetuate the memory of one who

made possible the development of vast lands and added beauty and charm to Riverside, Matthew Gage, canal builder. My father Ethan Allen Chase wrote the following in the *Riverside Daily Press* in 1892: "Matthew Gage was unknown, without friends and without means, empty handed and alone. He went forth and with his own good head, his sublime courage and his indomitable will, he triumphed over what to most men would have been insurmountable obstacles, and built the Gage Canal reclaiming nearly 8,000 acres of land, converting it into a fair and beautiful garden. This addition to Riverside over the first ten years had a valuation of over ten million dollars." [24]

Jane graciously thanked Harry Chase and his family, for the warm tribute to her husband and recalled his father's kind friendship. Jane Gage, age 80 years, died peacefully in her sleep several hours later that night. Her simple funeral was held in the Calvary Presbyterian Church and her cremains were placed in Olivewood Cemetery next to her husband and six children.[25] Her estate, administrated by her grandson, Gage Irving, consisted of two convertible notes, three bonds, and her house, valued at $6,500.

Matthew Gage's vision for Section 30 became a reality when the University of California developed his former land. Flourishing citrus groves transformed Section 30 into a phenomenal garden, a virtual "Garden of Eden," just as Matthew had proposed 47 years before.

EPILOGUE

ARLINGTON HOTEL
Renovated many times over the years and renamed The Riverside, it eventually became a residential hotel with 100 tenants before it burned to the ground in 1973.

CALVARY PRESBYTERIAN CHURCH
In 1931, the church made plans for larger facilities and purchased a three-acre parcel on the north side of the Tequesquite Arroyo from the Riverside School Board. Completed in 1936, the first services were held in the new house of worship at 4495 Magnolia Avenue in October. Additional improvements were constructed in 1940 and 1954.

CASA BLANCA TENNIS CLUB
When the sports club outlived its original purpose, the tennis clubhouse was utilized by a ladies' social club for many years. In 1966, the Church of Christ purchased the property for $18,500, razed the building, and built their new facility at 3601 Adams Street.

CHINATOWN
During the 1920s, occupants began to disappear and, by 1943, George Wong was the only resident and sole owner. His five acres became a dumping ground for abandoned cars and debris. Following his death in 1974, the property was sold and the buildings demolished. In the 1980s, an archaeological study by the Great Basin Foundation resulted in the publication of a detailed study of Riverside's Chinatown.

GAGE CANAL
The Tequesquite Arroyo flume was replaced with underground pipes in 1924. With inverted siphons and 14 pumping stations, the company continues to supply irrigation water to shareholders and will do so as long as necessary. In 1965, the Gage Canal Company and the City of Riverside entered into an agreement whereby stockholders would sell their Gage Canal shares to the city when their land no longer required irrigation. The city acquired considerable shares as agricultural land was converted to residential use.

MAGNOLIA AVENUE PRESBYTERIAN CHURCH
Enlarged and altered several times, the historic frame building has been preserved as a meeting hall. Presently the church is known as the Magnolia United Presbyterian Church, at 7200 Magnolia Avenue, and remains the oldest standing church in Riverside.

MATTHEW GAGE
His accomplishments have been recorded in local history books and the Gage Canal continues to perpetuate his name. In 1963, Matthew Gage Middle School opened at 6400 Lincoln Avenue in Arlington Heights, the area he developed and landscaped.

RIVERSIDE TRUST COMPANY, LIMITED
During World War I, the company experienced serious financial problems in meeting expenses and settling loans. By 1923, the company began liquidating its Riverside holdings and stockholders voted to dissolve the company in 1926. Subsequently, all records and accounting files were deliberately destroyed and for decades there have been mystifying stories and unfounded accusations about the Trust Company's management and or mismanagement.

SECTION 30
The Citrus Experiment Station, University of California, Riverside, encompasses most of Section 30 which is bisected by Iowa Avenue and Martin Luther King Jr. Boulevard. The facility is now known as the Citrus Research/Agricultural Experiment Station and is recognized as one of the foremost agricultural research centers in the world.

VICTORIA SCHOOL
With less than 10 students, the first Victoria School was demolished in 1919 and the school district returned the land and water stock to the Riverside Trust Company. Victoria Elementary School, at 2910 Arlington Avenue, opened in 1956 when Arlington Heights area contained more citrus trees than residents.

END NOTES

CHAPTER 1:
[1] Brown & Boyd, History of San Bernardino and Riverside Counties, Vol. 2, pg.715.
[2] Diary of Two Decades.
[3] *Riverside Press*, 1880s Advertisements.
[4] *Press & Horticulturist*, April 16, 1881.
[5] Ibid., January 8, 1881.
[6] Klotz & Hall, *Adobes, Bungalows, and Mansions of Riverside, California Revisited*, pg. 19.
[7] Ibid., pg. 20.
[8] Jane D. Gunther, *Riverside County, California, Place Names*.
[9] Brown & Boyd, *History of San Bernardino and Riverside Counties*, Vol. 2, pg. 604.
[10] *Riverside Daily Press*, November 4, 1939.
[11] *Press & Horticulturist*, March 31, 1883.
[12] Brown & Boyd, *History of San Bernardino and Riverside Counties*, Vol. 2, pg. 860.
[13] Great Basin Foundation, Vol. 2.
[14] *Press & Horticulturist*, September 3, 1881.

CHAPTER 2:
[1] *Press & Horticulturist*, January 7, 1882.
[2] J. A. Alexander, *The Life of George Chaffey*.
[3] *Press & Horticulturist*, April 15, 1882.
[4] Ibid., December 17, 1881.
[5] Ibid., January 21, 1882.
[6] Ibid., February 18, 1882.
[7] Ibid., March 4, 1882.
[8] Ibid., October 2, 1880.
[9] Ibid., March 20, 1883.
[10] Ibid., June 23, 1883.
[11] San Bernardino Records & Briefs, Vol. 2, Riverside Water Co. vs. Matthew Gage.
[12] *Press & Horticulturist*, March 25, 1882.
[13] Ibid., September 15, 1883.
[14] San Bernardino Archives, Box A, #2236.
[15] *Los Angeles Times*, November 27, 1883.
[16] Joan Hall, *A Citrus Legacy* pg. 14.
[17] *Press & Horticulturist*, October 17, 1883.
[18] San Bernardino Archives, Records and Briefs, Vol. 2, Riverside Water Company vs. Matthew Gage.

CHAPTER 3:
[1] Tom Patterson, *A Colony For California*, pg. 187.
[2] *Press & Horticulturist*, January 9, 1889.
[3] San Bernardino Recorder's Records, Deeds & Agreements, Hall Collection.
[4] Joan Hall, *A Citrus Legacy*, pg. 25.
[5] *Press & Horticulturist*, December 15, 1883.
[6] *Riverside Daily Press*, July 31, 1888.
[7] San Bernardino Archives, Records & Briefs Vol. 2, Riverside Water Company vs. Matthew Gage.
[8] *Press & Horticulturist*, June 13, 1885.
[9] San Bernardino Recorder's Records, Book of Agreements, T pg. 384.
[10] Joan Hall, *A Citrus Legacy*, pg. 26.
[11] Brown & Boyd, *History of San Bernardino and Riverside Counties*, Vol. 3, pg. 1224.
[12] Tom Patterson, *A Colony For California*, pg. 167.
[13] *Press & Horticulturist*, November 14, 1885.
[14] Wong Ho Leun Vol. 1, pg. 178.
[15] *Press & Horticulturist*, September 12, 1885.
[16] Ibid., January 9, 1886.
[17] *Riverside Daily Press*, February 4, 1888.
[18] Ibid., December 7, 1885.
[19] *Press & Horticulturist*, January 2, 1886.
[20] Los Angeles Land Office, Homestead Application # 6795.

CHAPTER 4:
[1] *Press & Horticulturist*, February 4, 1886.
[2] Ibid., January 9, 1886.
[3] Ibid., February 11, 1886.
[4] Ibid.
[5] *Press & Horticulturist*, December 5, 1885.
[6] San Bernardino County Records, March 18, 1886.
[7] *Press & Horticulturist*, June 24, 1886.
[8] Ibid., January 9, 1886.
[9] Ibid., October 1, 1887.
[10] Ibid., August 21, 1886.
[11] J. A. Alexander, *The Life of George Chaffey*.
[12] *Riverside Daily Press*, October 16. 1886.
[13] Ibid., October 9, 1886.
[14] *Press & Horticulturist*, November 13, 1886.
[15] S. H. Herrick Papers, Hall Collection.
[16] *Riverside Daily Press*, November 23, 1887.
[17] *Riverside Enterprise*, October 17, 1895.

18 *Press & Horticulturist*, May 28, 1887.
19 Klotz & Hall Adobes, *Bungalows and Mansions of Riverside*, pg. 41.
20 Tom Patterson, *A Colony For California*, pg. 173.
21 *Riverside Daily Press*, November 4, 1899.
22 *Riverside Daily Press*, June 25, 1887.
23 Ibid., July 2, 1887.
24 *Press & Horticulturist*, May 7, 1887.
25 Ibid., October 1, 1887.

CHAPTER 5:
1 *Riverside Daily Press*, February 4, 1888.
2 Brown & Boyd, *History of San Bernardino and Riverside Counties*, Vol. 3, pg. 1224.
3 *Riverside Daily Press*, April 2, 1888.
4 Ibid., May 28, 1888.
5 Ibid., February 9, 1887.
6 Ibid., March 17, 1888.
7 Ibid., August 14, 1888.
8 Stewart Malloch, Letter dated August 26, 1976.
9 *Press & Horticulturist*, October 1, 1887.
10 Ibid., December 15, 1888.
11 University of California Riverside, Rivera Library, Special Collections.
12 *Riverside Daily Press*, February 20, 1888.
13 Ibid., April 12, 1888.
14 William McGuigan, *Ventures In Faith*, pg. 29.
15 *Riverside Daily Press*, March 27, 1888.
16 *Press & Horticulturist*, September 22, 1888.
17 Ibid., October 29, 1888.
18 *Riverside Daily Press*, November 27, 1888.
19 University of California Riverside, Rivera Library, Special Collections.
20 *Press & Horticulturist*, September 7, 1889.

CHAPTER 6:
1 *Riverside Daily Press*, December 3, 1887.
2 Ibid., September 22, 1888.
3 *Press Enterprise*, October 14, 1984.
4 Ibid., January 12, 1970.
5 *Riverside Daily Press*, August 17, 1889.
6 Ibid., February 11, 1890.
7 Brown & Boyd, *History of San Bernardino and Riverside Counties*, Vol. 2, pg. 860.
8 *Riverside Daily Press*, April 6, 1890.
9 *Riverside Daily Press*, June 16, 1890.

[10] *Press & Horticulturist*, June 28, 1890.
[11] Ibid., January 29, 1891.
[12] *Riverside Daily Press*, August 9, 1890.
[13] Ibid., August 28, 1890.
[14] Ibid., November 30, 1891.
[15] Ibid., October 10, 1921.
[16] *Press & Horticulturist*, August 26, 1899.
[17] Tom Patterson, *A Colony for California*, pg. 244 - *Riverside Daily Press*, April 24, 1891.
[18] Historic American Engineering Record, 1991.
[19] *Press & Horticulturist*, December 5, 1891.
[20] Tom Patterson, *A Colony for California*, pg. 188.
[21] *Riverside Daily Press*, July 17, 1891.

CHAPTER 7:
[1] *Riverside Daily Press*, January 30, 1892.
[2] Glenn S. Dumke, *The Boom of the Eighties in Southern California*.
[3] *Riverside Daily Press*, May 10, 1892.
[4] Ibid., October 5, 1892.
[5] *Press & Horticulturist*, March 31, 1892.
[6] *Riverside Daily Press*, March 11, 1967.
[7] *Riverside Enterprise*, April 20, 1892.
[8] Ibid., August 3, 1893.
[9] Riverside Superior Court, Testimony of John Gunter, May 1899.
[10] History & Directory of Riverside County, 1893-4, Reprint, 1992.
[11] *Los Angeles Times*, April 13, 1893.
[12] Final Report, California at World's Columbian Exposition 1893. - *Riverside Daily Press*, May 22, 1894.
[13] *Riverside Enterprise*, October 17, 1895.
[14] *Arlington Times, Observations*, by Mrs. George Leibert, October 30, 1982.
[15] *Riverside Daily Press*, September 6, 1893.
[16] Ibid., October 7, 1893.
[17] Ibid., May 19-October 19, 1893.

CHAPTER 8:
[1] *Riverside Daily Press*, April 24, 1899.
[2] *Press & Horticulturist*, December 16, 1893.
[3] *Riverside Daily Press*, January 30, 1893.
[4] Ibid., June 13, 1893.
[5] Ibid., November 19, 1953.
[6] Ibid., August 18, 1894.
[7] Ibid., May 4, 1898.
[8] *Riverside Enterprise*, January 11, 1910.

[9] Riverside County Recorder's Office, Notice-October 15, 1895.
[10] *Riverside Enterprise*, October 17, 1895.
[11] *Press & Horticulturist*, June 1, 1895.
[12] *Adobes, Bungalows, and Mansions of Riverside*, Klotz & Hall, pg. 124.
[13] *Riverside Daily Press*, June 22-23, 1897.
[14] Ibid., August 3-4, 1897.
[15] Tom Patterson, *A Colony for California*, pg. 319.
[16] *Press & Horticulturist*, May 28, 1898.
[17] Ibid., June 18, 1898.
[18] *Riverside Daily Press*, December 9, 1898.
[19] *Riverside Enterprise*, May 30, 1899.

CHAPTER 9:
[1] *Press & Horticulturist*, January 5, 1889.
[2] *Riverside Enterprise*, May 30, 1899.
[3] Ibid.
[4] County of Riverside Superior Court Records Filed April 3, 1900.
[5] *Riverside Enterprise*, August 23, 1899.
[6] *Riverside Daily Press*, April 28, 1899.
[7] Ibid., April 30, 1898.
[8] Ibid., April 22, 1899.
[9] *Press & Horticulturist*, August 26, 1899.
[10] Ira Swett, *The Riverside & Arlington Electric Railway*.
[11] *Press & Horticulturist*, May 6, 1899.
[12] *Riverside Daily Press*, May 29, 1899.
[13] Ibid., March 2, 1900.
[14] *Riverside Enterprise*, August 15, 1899.
[15] Elmer W. Holmes, *History of Riverside County*, pg. 562.
[16] *Press & Horticulturist*, October 12, 1900.
[17] *Riverside Enterprise*, July 27, 1899.
[18] Ibid., December 27, 1899.

CHAPTER 10:
[1] Riverside City and County Directory, 1916.
[2] *Riverside Enterprise*, August 15, 1899.
[3] *Riverside Daily Press*, April 2, 1900.
[4] Ibid., March 2, 1900.
[5] Ibid., March 31, 1900.
[6] *Riverside Enterprise*, January 18, 1900.
[7] Esther Klotz, *Riverside and the Day the Bank Broke*, pg. 71.
[8] Tom Patterson, *A Colony for California*, pg. 144.
[9] *Press & Horticulturist*, December 11, 1897.
[10] *Press & Horticulturist*, November 27, 1900.

[11] *Riverside Enterprise,* November 27, 1900.
[12] Tom Patterson, *A Colony for California,* pg. 320.
[13] *Riverside Enterprise,* December 25, 1900.
[14] Klotz & Hall, *Adobes, Bungalows and Mansions of Riverside, Revisited,* pg. 147.
[15] *Riverside Enterprise,* January 17, 1901.
[16] *Riverside Daily Press,* January 28, 1901.
[17] *Riverside Enterprise,* February 2, 1901.
[18] Ibid., May 23, 1901.
[19] *Riverside Daily Press,* April 10, 1901.
[20] Ibid., April 29, 1902.
[21] Ibid., October 5, 1902.
[22] Tom Patterson, *A Colony for California,* pg. 323.
[23] *Riverside Enterprise,* December 21, 1902.
[23] *Riverside Daily Press,* July 3, 1905.
[24] Letter from M. Gage to T. Newton, January 28, 1904, Museum of Riverside Archives.
[25] Tom Patterson, *A Colony for California,* pg. 323.

CHAPTER 11:
[1] *Riverside Daily Press,* March 8, 1904.
[2] Ibid., March 9, 1904.
[3] Ibid., September 24-26, 1904.
[4] *Riverside Enterprise,* August 16, 1900.
[5] *Press &Horticulturist,* June 18, 1898.
[6] *Riverside Daily Press,* July 3, 1905.
[7] *Riverside Enterprise,* March 23, 1905.
[8] *Riverside Daily Press,* December 1, 1905.
[9] *Press & Horticulturist,* December 15, 1905.
[10] *Riverside Enterprise,* December 19, 1905.
[11] *Riverside Daily Press,* December 18, 1905.
[12] *Press & Horticulturist,* December 22, 1905.
[13] Ibid., December 15, 1905.
[14] Ibid., February 15, 1906.
[15] Ibid., April 18, 19, 20, 1906.
[16] Ibid., May 5, 1906.
[17] *Press & Horticulturist,* May 21, 1898.
[18] *Riverside Daily Press,* February 9, 1906.
[19] Ibid., December 24, 1906.
[20] *Riverside Enterprise,* November 3, 1906.
[21] *Riverside Daily Press,* April 10, 1907.
[22] Ibid., April 12, 1907.
[23] Ibid., October 30, 1907.

[24] *Press & Horticulturist*, December 22, 1905.
[25] *Riverside Daily Press*, April 8, 1909.
[26] Ibid., October 13, 1909.

CHAPTER 12:
[1] *Riverside Enterprise*, January 11, 1910.
[2] *Riverside Daily Press*, May 18, 1910.
[3] Ibid., May 19, 1910.
[4] Ibid., March 10, 1910.
[5] Ibid., February 28, 1911.
[6] Ibid., February 27, 1911.
[7] City of Riverside Directories, 1905-6.
[8] *Riverside Daily Press*, January 19, 1912.
[9] Ibid., June 20, 1912.
[10] Ibid.
[11] Ibid.
[12] Olivewood Cemetery Records.
[13] *Riverside Daily Press*, October 5, 1912.
[14] Ibid., December 16, 1912.
[15] Ibid., December 11, 1912.
[16] Ibid., December 30, 1912.
[17] Ibid., October 11, 1912.
[18] Ibid., January 2, 1912.
[19] Ibid., December 31, 1912.
[20] Ibid. December 30, 1912.

CHAPTER 13:
[1] *Los Angeles Times*, January 8, 1913.
[2] *Riverside Enterprise*, January 10, 1913.
[3] *Riverside Daily Press*, January 7, 1913.
[4] *Los Angeles Times*, January 6, 1913.
[5] *San Bernardino Daily Sun*, January 12, 1913.
[6] *Riverside Daily Press*, January 9, 1913.
[7] *Riverside Enterprise*, February 12, 1913.
[8] Ibid., February 18, 1913.
[9] *Riverside Daily Press*, February 17, 1913.
[10] *Los Angeles Times*, February 14, 1913.
[11] *Riverside Enterprise*, February 18, 1913.
[12] Ibid., February 19, 1913.
[13] Ibid., May 9, 1913.
[14] *Riverside Daily Press*, May 15, 1913.
[15] Ibid., June 19, 1913.
[16] Ibid., November 17, 1914.

¹⁷ Ibid., January 21, 1915.
¹⁸ Ibid., November 17, 1914.
¹⁹ *Riverside Enterprise*, November 17, 1914.

CHAPTER 14:
¹ *Riverside Enterprise*, November 17, 1914.
² Ibid., December 23, 1914.
³ *Riverside Daily Press*, December 23, 1914.
⁴ *Riverside Enterprise*, Deeds & Records, June 23, 1915.
⁵ *Riverside Daily Press*, June 19, 1915.
⁶ *Riverside Daily Press*, March 10-December 17, 1915.
⁷ *Riverside Enterprise*, February 17, 1915.
⁸ Ibid.
⁹ *Riverside Daily Press*, January 15, 1915.
¹⁰ *Riverside Enterprise*, November 9, 1915.
¹¹ Ibid.
¹² *Riverside Daily Press*, January 18, 1915.
¹³ *Riverside Enterprise*, January 24, 1916.
¹⁴ *Riverside Daily Press*, January 24, 1916.
¹⁵ Ibid.
¹⁶ *Riverside Enterprise*, January 24, 1916.
¹⁷ Ibid.
¹⁸ *Riverside Daily Press*, January 16, 1916.
¹⁹ Riverside County Clerks Records, County Courthouse.
²⁰ City of Riverside Directories, 1920s.
²¹ *Riverside Daily Press*, September 23, 1918.
²² Ibid., June 9, 1920.
²³ Olivewood Cemetery Records.
²⁴ *Riverside Daily Press*, April 1, 1929.
²⁵ Ibid., April 3, 1929.

BIBLIOGRAPHY

Alexander, J. A. *Life of George Chaffey*. London: MacMillan Company, 1928.

Bancroft, Herbert H. *The Book of the Fair-Columbian Exposition at Chicago 1893*. New York: Bounty Books, 1894.

Brown, John, Jr., and James Boyd. *History of San Bernardino and Riverside Counties*. Chicago: Western Historical Assn., Lewis Publishing Co., 1922. 3 vols.

Cooley, Bernice Bedford, *Dreamers, Dwellers, Ontario and Neighbors*. Privately Published, Riverside Public Library, 1982.

Dumke, Glenn S. *The Boom of the Eighties in Southern California*. San Marino, California: Huntington Library, 1944.

Elliott, Wallace W. *History of San Bernardino and Riverside Counties*, California. Riverside: Riverside Museum Press, 1965, Reprint.

Gabbert, John Raymond, *History of Riverside City and County*, Phoenix-Riverside: Record Publishing Company, 1935.

Greves, James P. *History of Riverside*. Riverside Public Library, Riverside, California.

Gunther, Jane Davies. *Riverside, California, Place Names*. Riverside: Rubidoux Printing Company, 1984.

Hall, Joan H. *A Citrus Legacy*. Riverside: Highgrove Press, 1992.

Hall, William H. *Irrigation-California*. Sacramento: State Printing Office, 1888.

Holmes, Elmer W. *A History of Riverside,* County. Los Angeles: Historic Record Company, 1912.

Leibert, Marie and Theresa Gordon, *Observations, Stories from the Arlington Times.* Self Published, 1983.

Lech, Steve, *Along the Old Roads, A History of the Portion of Southern California That Became Riverside County.* Self Published, 2004.

McGroarty, John Steven. *California of the South.* Chicago, Los Angeles, Indianapolis: S. J. Clarks Publishing Co., 1933.

McGuigan, William. *Ventures in Faith, Calvary Presbyterian Church Riverside, California, 1887-1987.* Self-Published, 1987.

Patterson, Tom. *A Colony for California.* Riverside: Press-Enterprise, 1971.

Patterson, Tom. *Landmarks of Riverside.* Riverside: Press-Enterprise Company, 1964.

Robinson, W. W., *Panorama, A Picture History of Southern California.* Los Angeles: Title Insurance and Trust Company. 1953.

Rudisill, Henry J., *Riverside, A City Among the Orange Groves.* Riverside: Board of Trade, 1889.

Spalding, William Andrew, *The Orange: Its Culture in California.* Riverside Press-Horticulturist. 1885.

Swett, Ira. *The Riverside and Arlington Electric Railway,* Los Angeles: I. L. Swett Company, 1962.

Wong Ho Leum, *An American Chinatown.* San Diego: The Great Basin Foundation, 1987, 2 vols.

NEWSPAPERS, DOCUMENTS, PAMPHLETS AND ARTICLES

Arlington Times

London Times

Los Angeles Times

New York Times

Riverside Daily Press

Riverside Enterprise

Riverside Press & Horticulturist

Riverside Weekly News

San Bernardino Daily Sun

San Bernardino Sun Telegram

San Diego Sun

San Francisco Chronicle

California *Citrograph*, July 1914-February 1991.

Calvary Presbyterian Church Archives.

Census of the United States, 1880, 1900, 1910.

Court Cases: San Bernardino County Records & Briefs.

Riverside County Court Clerks Probate Records.

Riverside County Recorders Records.

Deeds and Agreements of Matthew Gage, San Bernardino County Recorders Office, Hall Collection.

Diary of Two Decades: Riverside Events 1875-1882. Reprint in *Press & Horticulturist*.

East Riverside Water Company, Articles of Incorporation, Hall Collection.

Evergreen Cemetery Records.

Historic American Engineering Record, Victoria Bridge, 1991.

History and Directory of Riverside County, 1893-4. Historical Commission, 1992.

History of Arlington Heights by Stewart Malloch, letter dated 1976.

Information and interviews with Mr. and Mrs. John Mylne and Mrs. Robert Irving regarding Gage and Irving family histories.

Olivewood Cemetery Records.

Riverside Cultural Heritage Board, City Landmarks, March 2005.

Riverside Directories, 1889 to 1930

San Bernardino Artesian Basin, by Frederick C. Finkle, series of articles in San Bernardino Sun-Telegram beginning October 19, 1947.

Sanborn Fire Company, Sanborn Map Company, 1884-5. United States Department of the Interior Geological Survey, Department of Water, Facilities in Santa Ana River Basin, California, 1810-1968. M. B. Scott Menlo Park, California.

Water Facilities in Santa Ana River Basin, 1810-1968, California Department of Water Resources, San Bernardino Valley Municipal Water District, Western Municipal Water District of Riverside County.

ACKNOWLEDGEMENTS

This book could not have been completed without the support of many people and their helpful contributions. For years I have benefited from the resources of the Riverside Public Library and most recently Dominque McCafferty, Ruth, Mary, Cathy, and Bruce Burton have been most accommodating.

I am also indebted to Alan Curl for his skillful editing and valuable suggestions that greatly improved the text. My thanks to Kevin Hallaran, Riverside Metropolitan Museum Archivist, for locating specific photographs and supplying information that helped the story line. I am most grateful to Robin Hanks for her expertise in formatting text and photos and for the encouragement generated by her husband, Richard.

I especially thank Terry (John M.) Mylne, and his wife, B.J., who graciously made available family histories and photos of the Gage and Irving families that greatly enhanced the story involving his family's lineage.

And lastly, I am most appreciative for the advice and guidance offered by my husband, Howard. His knowledge of citrus culture and his many contributions enabled me to record the challenges, conquests, and calamities of Matthew Gage.

Joan H. Hall, 2008

ABOUT THE AUTHOR

Joan Hall and Robin Hanks at a book signing during the
Old Riverside Foundation Annual Home Tour in 2011

Joan had been publishing books for years and had her own publishing company, Highgrove Press, but she had always relied on the printers do the layout as well as the printing. In 2007, I made a proposal to layout her newest manuscript on Matthew Gage and she accepted it. Joan had definite opinions about how things should be, so we often worked together in her "cloffice," as Nancy Parrish affectionately called it, in the closet of her guest room. When it came time to look for photographs and do more research, we worked with Kevin Hallaran, who was a longtime friend of Joan's. Kevin's invaluable assistance not only made this book possible, but all of Joan's future books as well. We solicited bids on the printing in April of 2008 and we kept to Joan's small runs of 500 books.

Joan liked to deal with local printers, so by late July 2008 we finally decided on Acrey and Tharp Printing. Dave Tharp was quite a character and he convinced us to print the books in soft cover, so we had to rework the files. Joan asked me to design the cover of *Pursuing Eden*, which was an honor, and after that the work progressed at Dave's pace. Joan was a keen marketer, so her goal was to have the book out by Christmas. We had our book signing at Barnes & Noble in the Galleria at Tyler in Riverside on December 6, 2008.

Something I discovered about Joan was that she always had to have something to do. Over the next year, Joan worked on her new manuscript and for much of 2010 she and I were researching, collecting photographs and laying out her next book, *Riverside's Invisible Past*. She had published a soft cover version of this book in 1979, but this time she wanted a coffee table, hard cover book.

At the September 9, 2010 RMA Board meeting Joan offered to donate the copyright of her book, *Riverside's Invisible Past*, to the Riverside Museum Associates. She requested that they publish the book using funds from the RMA Press with the stipulation that the proceeds they receive from the sales of the book replenish the Press account so that those funds will still be available for future publishing. All additional proceeds after repaying the Press account will go to the RMA general fund to aid in their continuing support of the museum and its programs. The beautiful hard cover *Riverside's Invisible Past* was published in late November 2010. It was sure to become a collector's item in the not too distant future.

Joan's next book project was the story of Jonathan Tibbet, an early champion of the rights of Southern California Indians. She spent countless hours researching and writing his story and during this time she decided she wanted to retire her publishing company. I decided to start Coyote Hill Press and she walked me though the process of setting up a DBA, putting the press releases in the newspaper, buying

ISBN numbers, and all the elements of establishing my own publishing company. In 2014, two of the first books published by Coyote Hill Press were *Vermont's Proper Son* by Richard A. Hanks and *Riverside's One & Only Buffalo Heart* by Joan H. Hall. Joan did the indexes for both her book and Richard's, which she did by hand on 3x5 cards, because Joan felt that an accurate index was critical to the success of a scholarly work.

In March 2018, Joan and I decided we were going to publish *A Riverside Dynasty* and sell it at the Old Riverside Foundation Home Tour at the Rumsey house. We worked in secret until we were sure we could pull this off and on April 18th I received this email from her: "Hi Robin first draft arrived - working on corrections and index- hope to get it back to you over weekend so you can more or less put it to bed before your trip to So Cal how long do you think it will take to publish and have in hand? palz Joan." By that Friday she sent me her corrections, and a few days later the acknowledgments and index.

We later had lots of laughs over Howard helping her download the files to a flash drive and get it printed at PIP --that was more technology than Howard had ever had to deal with. But Joan was adamant about correcting mistakes and she assured me that even though she was having eye problems she could find mistakes because she had magnifying glasses in every room. Joan was thrilled to receive ten finished copies a few weeks later that she could give away to all those who had helped her.

In June 2018, Richard and I spent the afternoon with Howard and Joan and they told us all about their beginnings in Riverside, early water rights and the adventures of inheriting orange groves. I never met anyone quite like Joan Hall and I am so proud to have been a part of this woman's life and to have helped her publish many of her greatest works. With the blessing of her three sons, Coyote Hill Press will continue to keep her legacy alive by reprinting *Pursuing Eden* and distributing the book to local Riverside book stores and gift shops.

Joan Herrick Hall passed away on July 19, 2018 and Howard Gilbert Hall followed her a year and a half later on November 22, 2019. Both are buried at Evergreen Memorial Park in Riverside, California.

Robin S. Hanks, 2023

INDEX

D

Deere, George H. Reverend, 125
Desert Land Act, 20, 64, 140, 141, 143,
Dingley Bill, 134
Diphtheria, 111, 112, 114
Dyer, O. T., 38, 45, 62, 94, 123

E

Earthquakes, 25, 151, 152, 177, 178,
Edgemont, 163, 164, 172
Electricity, 48, 78, 135, 209,
Entry Men, see also Atwater, Gunther, Newman, 51, 81, 119, 138, 154
Etiwanda Colony, 18, 22, 28, 46, 60, 78
Evans, Samuel C., 9, 60, 189, 209, 211, 212, 213, 216
Evergreen Cemetery, 16, 75, 92, 190, 208, 218

F

Forbes, C. F. Reverend, 21

G

Gage, Anna, xiii, 220,
Gage Canal, xi, 33, 48, 50, 55, 57, 59, 63, 67, 69, 70, 76, 81, 84, 87, 92, 97, 99, 108, 114, 125, 131, 135, 137, 157, 158, 166, 171, 180, 183, 184, 215, 217, 220, 223
Gage, Edith Anna, xiii, 16
Gage, Frances Gibson, xiii, 71, 80, 91, 107, 113
Gage, Henry B. Reverend, 68, 107
Gage, Horace James, xiii, 1, 7, 13, 20, 23, 32, 39, 59, 71, 80, 85, 91, 107, 112

Gage, Jane Gibson, xiii, 22, 61, 106, 164, 165, 174, 176, 177, 180, 186, 193, 214, 217, 221, 222
Gage, Katherine MacKenzie, xiii, 97, 98, 173, 194
Gage, Margaret Jane, xiii, 1, 221
Gage, Margaret Jane Orr, xiii, 53, 75, 78, 107,
Gage, Mary Margaret, (Mrs. William John), xiii, 68, 69, 83
Gage, Mary Irving (Mrs. Robert), xiii, 68, 171
Gage, Matthew, ii, ix-xiii, 1, 5, 10, 12, 17, 19-22, 25, 26, 27, 28, 30, 34, 35, 36, 38, 43-52, 54-56, 58, 59, 62-64, 66-70, 72, 75, 79-82, 84-92, 94, 95, 97, 99, 104, 106, 108, 109, 112, 113, 115, 123, 125, 126-129, 133, 134, 137, 138, 140, 143, 146-150, 153, 154, 155, 157, 158-161, 165, 167, 169, 171, 173, 175, 176, 180, 181, 182, 183, 185, 186, 190, 191, 193, 195, 197, 204, 205, 212, 214-218, 221, 222, 224
Gage, Maude Louise, xiii, 1, 4, 6, 11, 13, 14, 20, 23, 27, 32, 39, 59, 71, 80, 85, 107, 109, 110, 124, 125, 137, 162, 164, 165, 169, 170, 172, 183, 190, 204, 218, 220, 221
Gage, Robert, xiii, 17, 27, 37, 56, 69, 70, 79, 97, 99, 112, 137, 146, 147, 151, 163, 171, 193
Gage, Robert Condit, xiii, 27, 111
Gage, William John, xiii, 37, 112, 193, 217
Garcia, J. S., 17, 28
Glenwood Cottage, 3-5, 8, 10, 11, 13, 26, 35, 123
Glenwood Hotel, 26, 49, 82, 85, 87, 89, 92, 95, 96, 97, 102, 135, 151, 154, 156, 159, 173
Glenwood Mission Inn, 168, 173, 183, 188, 197

Society, 188, 190, 214, 215
Perrine, C. O., 63, 84
Price, Waterhouse & Company, 35, 90, 203
Price, Samuel - Edwin Waterhouse, 90

Q

Queen Victoria, 14, 58, 78, 80, 133, 134, 163

R

Raeburn, 80, 131, 132, 137, 147, 162, 170, 188
Railroads,
  California Southern, 89, 123
  Central & Southern Pacific, 27
  Riverside, Santa Ana, & Los Angeles, 45, 47, 53, 56, 79
  Santa Fe, 115, 209, 218
  Southern Pacific, 30, 197
  Union Pacific, 1
Reed, John Henry, 205, 206, 209, 216
Riverside & Arlington Railroad (R&A), 148, 158, 178
Riverside Banking Company, 38, 45, 60, 62, 123
Riverside Baptist Church, 21
Riverside County, 117, 139, 166, 197
Riverside County Courthouse, 138, 153, 180, 182
Riverside Fruit Company, 164
Riverside Fruit Exchange, 122, 160
Riverside Golf & Polo Club, 109
Riverside Heights Water Company, 48
Riverside High School, 125
Riverside Land & Irrigating Company, 4, 9, 60

Riverside Orange Company, 114, 160, 174
Riverside Police Shooting, 194-196
Riverside Street Fair 1900, 156, 157
Riverside Trust Company, Limited, 92, 93, 98, 99, 101, 103, 104, 108, 114, 116, 126, 127, 128, 137, 145, 146, 147, 151, 158, 159, 166, 168, 173, 174, 176, 178, 181, 182, 185, 186, 203, 204, 224
Riverside Water Canal, 12, 36, 46, 47, 78, 82
Riverside Water Company, 36, 46, 47, 55, 59, 64, 66, 69, 70, 82, 128, 158, 159, 184, 185
Roe, James, 9, 21, 158
Roe's Drug Store, 5, 9, 10, 11, 12, 17, 45, 158
Rosenthal, Emil, 66, 67
Rubidoux Hotel, 66, 123
Rumsey, Cornelius, 161, 162, 190

S

San Bernardino, 2, 10, 16, 17, 20, 23, 24, 25, 31, 40, 43, 44, 46, 51, 53, 54, 55, 57, 58, 59, 66, 70, 79, 80, 87, 93, 117, 151, 180
San Francisco Six Companies, 47, 121
San Jacinto Tin Mines, 98, 125
Santa Ana Canyon, 39
Santa Ana River, 2, 22, 23, 24, 25, 28, 29, 31, 39, 40, 43, 49, 55, 58, 69, 70, 99, 130, 216
Satterwaite Act, 18, 62
Scotia Place, 21
Section 30, xi, 20, 21, 22, 23, 28, 32, 34, 35, 36, 38, 39, 43, 45, 48, 49, 51, 52, 56, 60, 62, 63, 64, 67, 68, 80, 81, 90, 91, 93, 113, 114, 118, 119, 125, 129, 130, 131, 133, 138 139, 140, 141, 142, 143, 144, 145,

146, 150, 153, 154, 155, 161, 165, 166, 173, 180, 181, 186, 190, 199 201, 204, 205, 208, 212, 213, 215 219, 220, 221, 222, 224
Sherman Antitrust Act, 137
Smallpox, (Pest House), 68, 72, 119
Smith, Hoke, 129, 153
Sneath, George, 90, 92
Southern California Colony Association, 2, 23
Southern California Fruit Exchange 122
Spaulding, William, 77
Spooner, Robert, 79
Spooner, Sarah Gage, 64, 69, 95, 215, 218
Stewart, J. B. Reverend, 69, 83, 84
Streeter, Henry, 117

T

Taft, William Howard President, 183, 189
Temescal Tin Mines, 61
Tequesquite Arroyo, 29, 41, 46, 52, 60, 62, 63, 67, 71, 73, 74, 75, 80, 81, 93, 97, 103, 158
Tequesquite Trestle, 75
Tetley, Frank, 166, 167, 181
Tetley Hotel, 167, 201
Thompson, G. Howard, 172, 180, 181, 182, 186
Tibbets, Luther, 157
Twogood, Adoniran Judson, 28, 42, 43, 44, 56, 59, 77, 94, 122, 137
Twogood, Daniel C., 77, 122
Twogood Nursery, 77

U

University of California - Citrus Experiment Station, 206, 207, 220

V

Victoria Avenue, 80, 81, 93, 97, 101, 102, 104, 108, 109, 114, 131, 159, 161, 162, 166, 170, 175, 178, 179 188
Victoria Bridge, 103, 104, 106, 158, 178
Victoria Club, 169, 178, 194, 219
Victoria School, 108, 109, 224
Victoria Tract, 58, 92, 98, 138

W

Waterhouse, Theodore, 90, 92
Water Witch, 48
Webber, Herbert John, 204, 210, 213
White, Albert S., 81
White's Addition, 48, 67, 81
Williams, Fannie Doctor, 85
Winterbotham, William H., 203, 204
Women's Christian Temperance Union, 102
Woodill, Alfred Doctor, 2, 3, 4, 5, 6, 15, 21, 32, 38, 45, 69, 75

Y

Young Men's Christian Association, 85, 92

COYOTE HILL PRESS

CAMANO ISLAND, WA